Simple Path to Wealth

Your Guide to Financial Freedom

E.A. Sparks

Table of Contents

Introduction

Money can make life miserable. That may sound strange but it's true. If you don't have the right mindset about money, you can indeed feel overpowered by it. That's how millions of people out there feel because they have no clue how to make peace with their finances. Everybody wants to be in a position where they don't have to go to work every single day and just wait for the paycheck at the end of the month to be able to pay all sorts of bills and then again get back to the same cycle. But that's how life is for most of us. We know we need more money to be able to get out of debt, to be able to afford the things that may seemingly improve or upgrade our lives, and to have more time and freedom to live life on our own terms.

You know what? No matter how much you wrestle with the idea of making more money and becoming wealthy one day, it's not going to take you anywhere. The reason is quite simple—it's *you* who has to change your attitude toward money for the situation to turn around. The power to master money is within you. There's nothing that can stop you from creating wealth and becoming financially independent. Whether it's the overbearing debt obligations, feeble credit history, or a meager paycheck every month, none of it has the power to take away what you can do to live debt-free, have more money in your bank account, fulfill all your dreams, and look forward to a fulfilling retirement.

You haven't been able to get on the path of wealth creation so far because you haven't taken charge of your finances yet. You've lived unaware, enslaved, and deterred by money. But it's never too late. You can change your financial destiny as long as you're willing to educate yourself about how to manage your finances, stay out of debt, and make your money grow. The rules of money are the same for everyone. Whether you're born rich or poor, employed with the best of companies or earn a small salary, every single person can lose or create money. It's all about what you think of money and how you treat it.

To begin with, you need to understand that money is just a medium, which is meant to facilitate you. Thus, you don't need to get controlled by it. When people allow money to control them, they live worried and anxious about how they're going to pay the next set of bills and they often feel drowned in the uncertainty of the future. On the other hand, when you learn to control money, you live peacefully and aren't scared of what's coming ahead. So, how do you achieve that? Well, that's exactly what this book is going to unveil for you.

You need to think about your personal finances like a project of your life, which will help you handle money strategically. The reason why most people spend money wastefully and pay high interest on their credit cards is because they aren't aware of the easier and smarter way to meet their needs and desires. They want to live in the moment and gratify their impulsive whims and fancies, not realizing they're accumulating bad debt, which is hard to pay back. When people think about the idea of spending carefully and saving for the future, it makes them feel as if they're going to miss out on something fun or their peers might get ahead of them. But that's not true. You can afford anything you like and have a more enriching life if you simply get conscious about your spending and take your future into perspective, which is why you need certain financial goals. While everybody does think about buying a house, traveling, and retiring someday, they don't know the path to get there.

However, the path is right there ahead of you. All you need is a little bit of understanding, knowledge, and willingness to improve your finances, in order to see it. The day you begin to feel accountable about your money and implement a plan as to how you'd like to spend that money, save for retirement, and also look for ways to channel it to work for you, there's nothing that can keep you from creating wealth.

You don't have to feel overwhelmed by your finances because it's your own choices that direct the course of your financial trajectory. You simply need to believe in yourself and become more self-aware to change your financial destiny. After you've read this book, you'll know how to manage your money so that it's never scarce. You'll learn the importance of making investments and growing your financial assets. You'll understand that stock market and cryptocurrency are not scary terms, and they're definitely not a gamble. Anybody can develop expertise to invest their money and make it work for them. There's huge money to be made through real estate investments, which most people assume is out of reach for them. Apart from that, you'll also learn about how an additional source of income can help you get out of debt faster and aid in your financial progress. It's never a bad idea to want to make more money because it contributes toward your financial stability. Remember, we don't want to make oodles of money to compete with somebody else or to be able to surpass our peers. We want to have enough money to savor the quality of life.

There's nothing wrong in desiring more freedom of time to be able to go after goals that truly matter. When you don't have to worry about paying debt, it gives your mind mental peace and you're able to enjoy your relationships better and nurture all the meaningful things in life. Money is definitely the key to the way we shape our lives. The good news is that you can take action toward not allowing money to go out of your pocket inadvertently. You can decide to fix your gaze on the future and all the dreams that you'd like to realize someday, which will empower you to work toward building wealth.

So, are you ready to get ahead of the pitfalls of money and attain wealth?

Chapter 1: Money Management

"The more your money works for you, the less you have to work for money."
–Idowu Koyenikan

The foundation of good finances is managing money wisely. There's no other formula or a recipe for creating wealth. It's a relationship you need to share with the money you earn that motivates you to build it. If you aren't aware of where your money is going every month, you'll always be clueless about your finances as a whole. It's the simple things that really make a big difference to how things take their course. The difference between those who budget and those who don't is not really the income or inheritance they have, but it's the confidence and assurance of knowing their finances. You need to come to terms with your money. How do you do that? Well, that's where budgeting and tracking your expenses come into the picture.

Start Budgeting

Whether you like it or not, budgeting is an integral aspect of building a strong financial future. So, you better embrace it for your own good. You can make lots of money but it's going to sustain you only when you manage it prudently. There are all kinds of budgeting styles to pick and choose from. The end goal is to spend consciously and save for the future. The purpose of budgeting is to train your mind to take charge of money and not let it enslave you. Thus, each person should start budgeting as soon as they start earning. The sooner you begin, the earlier you can establish a solid financial base for yourself.

The 50/30/20 Method of Budgeting

With the 50/30/20 budgeting method, you can really structure your finances and know exactly how you want to use your money. This method doesn't just allow you to spend on your desires, it ensures that you have enough money to pay for all your necessities every month. In addition, you still have money left for debt repayment and to allocate toward future savings.

Let's examine how this works:

To implement the 50/30/20 budget, you need to first know your net income/after-tax income and then decide to spend 50% of it on your needs, 30% on your wants or desires, and use the remaining 20% to pay off your outstanding credit card balances, mortgage, or loans, as well as to fund your savings. Now, how much you want to use for debt repayment and how much for savings depends on how much debt you have. If you have quite a lot of debt, paying it off on priority makes more sense. Once you're out of debt or at least have reduced the burden to a great extent, you can begin boosting your savings.

Now, you also need to categorize your expenses, meaning list down your necessities and wants to be able to take advantage of this budgeting strategy. Don't confuse wants with needs. If you feel like buying a new pair of shoes for a party, it's a desire and not a necessity. On the other hand, paying your rent, buying groceries, and paying your electricity or water bill are all absolute necessities. Then, there are also fixed and variable expenses like the amount you pay to your landlord which is not going to change; however, you don't have to shell out the same amount of money on groceries every month.

Track Your Spending

The best part about budgeting is that it compels you to monitor your spending. You're no longer unaware of where your money is going. For instance, if you've set a particular budget for eating out every month, it's going to help you spend within a limit. Paying attention to your spending also brings to your notice your unnecessary expenses, such as excessive coffees, all kinds of subscriptions, and shopping.

To track your expenses, you need to first list them down and categorize them. For example, you can mention gas, electricity, and water under the main category called utilities, and then write things like toilet paper, laundry detergent, pasta, cereal, and bread under groceries. The best way to find out where you end up spending all your money each month is to pull out your bank and credit card statements. Then, get all the receipts and bills.

Don't Spend More Than You Earn

The purpose of paying attention to your expenses is to know if you're spending more than your income. When people operate without a budget, they usually tend to overspend, which is the root cause of debt and lack of savings. The only way you can develop the habit of expending money within your means is by following a budget.

You may have to make a few conscious choices to control your spending:

- The first thing you can do is reduce eating out and ordering food. Instead, try to cook your own meals at least a few times in a week.

- Always shop for things you need and not the things that catch your fancy out of the blue. Also, don't pick up something just because it's available at a discounted price.

- Cut down on giving your clothes to the dry cleaner. Wash them yourself.

- Choose to walk small distances instead of taking your car every time.

- Make sure you aren't wasting electricity, gas, and water.

- Find alternatives to weekend clubbing or going out. You may want to go hiking in the forest, which is more beneficial for your health and isn't an expensive activity.

- Try to upcycle the things you already have instead of rushing to buy new ones.

Set Financial Goals

When you know why you want to limit your expenses, it becomes easier to align your thoughts and willingness to save. If your mind tells you to squander money and live in the moment, you can remind yourself of your future self and the things you'd like to achieve. Everybody has certain financial goals they want to accomplish, such as studying abroad, owning a house, or traveling to a new country. There are goals you want to achieve within a few months or maybe a year, and then there are long-term goals that you want to reach in a span of 8 to 10 years.

Retirement is everyone's ultimate goal, which they may or may not be serious about. Some people begin to fund their retirement savings right from the start while some don't realize its importance until they turn 40.

Financial goals give you clarity about how you want to live your life and also how much money you need to fulfill everything you want to have. However, you need to set realistic goals by using the guideline below:

- Be very specific about your goals. If you simply want to have more money but have no idea what you want to do with it, you will not be able to discipline your mind about money. You should pick specific targets like paying off your debt, buying a car, or moving to a new city.

- Fix an amount that you want to work toward. For example, if you want to pay off your student loan, you need to decide on a particular amount you want to separate each month for debt repayment.

● Then, you need to know the time it's going to take to reach that milestone. For instance, if you want to get rid of a loan, you need to know the end date of that loan.

● Lastly, it's important to realize that your goals should be based on your own personal beliefs and values. Your goals should give you a sense of purpose in life, meaning you should feel excited about them. If you simply get influenced by somebody else and try to achieve what they want to do, it's not going to work for you. If somebody else wants to buy a farmhouse and retire at 35, you don't have to follow in their footsteps.

● In order to prioritize your financial goals, you need to write them down. When you simply talk about what you want to achieve, it fizzles away in the noise of everyday mundanity. However, penning down your goals imprints them on your mind and keeps reminding you to take action toward them.

Make Sacrifices

While we live in the age of consumerism and it's challenging to ignore the attractive propositions that are laid before us, we can still make certain choices to improve our finances.

Below are some of the sacrifices that can help your finances take a big leap over time:

● Keeping one car for many years.
● Moving to a cheaper house.
● Delaying marriage and starting a family.
● Ending friendships with toxic/negative people.
● Cutting down on shopping, entertainment, and vacationing.
● Abandoning non-productive hobbies/pastimes.
● Getting out of bed early to get more accomplished through the day.

When you let go of your material desires for a few years, you're in a much stronger financial position to buy anything you like later. The beauty of giving up on the things that give you only momentary pleasure and no real reward is that you stop chasing them after you reach a certain stage in life. As you grow older and gain more wisdom, you know what truly matters and how to make your life more fulfilling.

The most important of all sacrifices is to discard your impulsive ways and practice self-control. When you begin to work on your habits and the choices you make every day, it has an impact on your overall success. Remember, people who are not able to build wealth often make poor choices. They procrastinate on things they're supposed to do and spend more time in activities that have no fruitful outcome. So, you need to constantly work toward becoming who you want to be and stop being the person who hinders your progress.

Practice Self-Discipline

Discipline is a close cousin of sacrifice. When you commit to managing your money in a certain way no matter what happens, it demonstrates your financial discipline. The two main pillars of financial discipline are spending below your income and fostering good financial habits like budgeting, avoiding debt, saving, and investing. People who think long-term and want to plan for their future self know how to incorporate self-discipline.

Below are some of the examples of self-discipline in regard to finances:

- Automate your savings and pay yourself first. You need to put away at least a certain portion of your net income each month in a separate savings account and never touch it. You don't have to pay your bills or go shopping the moment you get your paycheck. The first thing you need to do is deduct 20% (or more) of it and direct it toward your emergency savings, retirement funds, and all sorts of other short-term, mid-term, or long-term savings.

- Don't buy something you don't need. Try your level best to delay your purchases and allow time for self-analysis. Think over why you want to buy something and if it really makes a difference to your life.

- Educate yourself on personal finance management. Read books, watch TV shows, browse YouTube channels, and listen to podcasts that offer knowledge and insights on wealth creation. Learn about how to budget, how to save and invest, and how to stay out of debt.

Controlling your expenses and saving may sound like you're depriving yourself of the pleasures of life, but when you stick to spending way less than you'd like to, you have more freedom to live the way you like and have no fear of the future.

Watch Your Credit Card Use

Most people don't know the right use of a credit card. They take it as a means to buy anything they feel like even at the cost of building an unmanageable amount of debt. The way people use credit cards has given them a reputation that they're evil to use, which isn't actually true. In fact, you can use credit cards to your advantage and build credit. You don't have to get into debt. People get into debt because they begin using credit cards without any financial education. They aren't aware how interest rates work and why it's better to pay your balances in full each billing cycle.

In order to take charge of how you use your credit card, you need to understand its very purpose and then ensure that it's helping you grow financially and not pushing you back. You need to be aware that the credit you're given is to facilitate you in making certain important purchases quickly rather than waiting for the day when you have the required amount. For instance, you can buy an electronic item or a home appliance with the help of a credit card and also earn reward points. There's no problem using a credit card, as long as you don't carry balances and fail to make all your payments on time. It's only when you carry high balances that you need to pay interest in addition to the principal amount that you owe. Also, if you make late payments or miss them completely, there are additional fees that are charged.

If you use credit cards in a controlled manner, it can help you maintain a good credit history. When you have a high credit rating, you're eligible to avail credit on low interest rates and flexible loan terms. Creditors trust borrowers who have long-standing records of timely payments and those who utilize limited credit. On the other hand, people who use excessive credit and don't pay it back within a reasonable time period find it hard to convince lenders for easy credit terms.

Credit isn't bad at all. It's meant to propel your financial efforts. However, it takes a bad shape when it turns into debt. It's in your hands if you want to carry debt or pay it off as quickly as possible. Credit cards are your baseline that set you up for the rest of your credit journey. If you learn to use your credit cards wisely, you can handle other debts smartly, too.

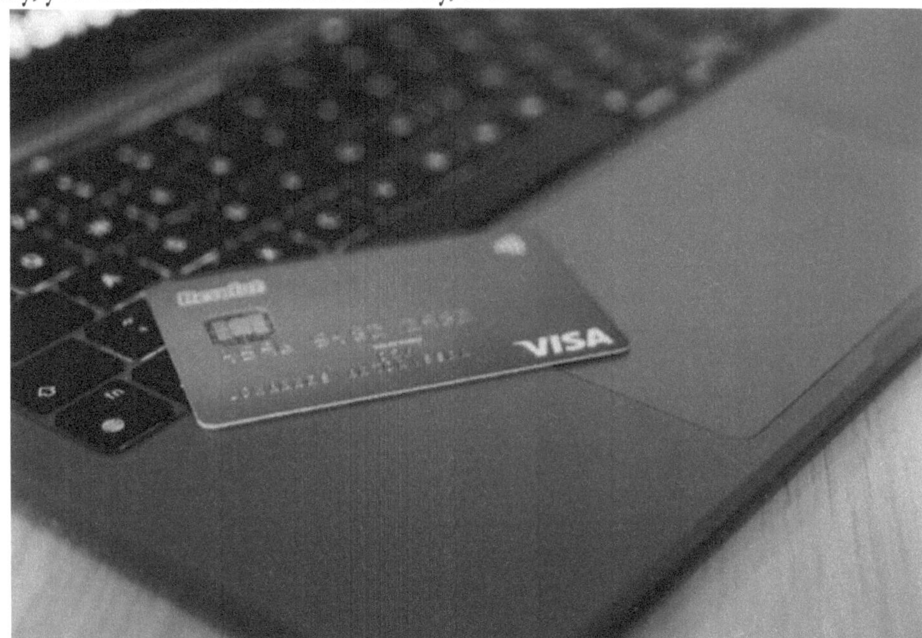

With the foundation of good credit history, you can take advantage of mortgage, student loans, and various other kinds of loans. When you take credit to own real estate, it's a step toward making more money in the long run. Similarly, when you take out a loan to upgrade your education or start a new business venture, it's a step forward into increasing your earning potential. So, you need to think about what's giving you a return and what isn't. The consumer goods that you buy with your credit card are of depreciating value, and thus, they have no return. However, the credit you avail to buy a house or invest in a new career allows you to grow and unlock new opportunities.

Money management skills aren't tough to acquire. You need to begin with writing down your life goals and then thinking about how you want to achieve them. Make an actionable plan, which has to include following a budget and cutting down on expenses. You shouldn't be afraid to make certain sacrifices and commit to saving money to be able to enjoy more freedom and flexibility in the future. Credit cards are supposed to make shopping convenient for you, but you need to draw a line somewhere and never let debt get too high.

The foundation of good financial health for any individual lies in their financial awareness and knowledge. If you don't have your own perspective on money, you'll simply get influenced by what others are doing and end up making wrong financial decisions. Thus, you need to work on your financial literacy, which we are going to uncover in the next chapter.

Chapter 2: Financial Literacy

"The lack of money is the root of all evil." –Mark Twain

When you don't have enough, your mind is preoccupied with thoughts of wanting more and it hinders you from achieving more. Living for a paycheck is the most pitiful thing to do, yet most people are doing exactly that. They have no clue what their future holds. All they're focused on is how to survive the next month, how to pay the bills, and where to go shopping. No matter how much people earn, they aren't really happy. There are only a few who are truly satisfied with their jobs. Why is that? Have you thought about it?

We all work for money. If we don't, we won't be able to pay rent, college fees, buy groceries, and fund other mandatory expenses. Money is important and that's why people take up jobs even when they don't like them at all. The conventional idea about money tells you to go to a place and report to somebody every day. Your entire life is dependent on the salary that you receive at the end of each month. What people don't realize is that when you limit yourself in a job, you stop growing as an individual. Thus, your focus should be on honing your skills and not just drawing a paycheck.

Work for Skill Enhancement

The day you begin to think differently about why you want to work, your capability to make more money will increase. When you work for a paycheck, you get stuck in it. However, when you work to learn new things and upgrade your skills, you open a whole new arena of opportunities for yourself. Therefore, you should choose your job carefully and not settle for anything that comes your way. People who work for the sake of working don't enjoy their jobs and they fail to realize their true potential. On the other hand, those who are passionate about their work and keep enhancing their expertise and knowledge end up making real progress. They are able to expand their earning capacity and reach new levels of success.

You shouldn't run after money because it's going to decrease in value over time due to inflation, which is unavoidable. However, your financial awareness and knowledge will enable you to know how to create abundant wealth and overpower the rising prices. When you seek to learn and grow, money comes by automatically. It's a byproduct of skill enhancement. In fact, it comes more quickly and easily. The purpose behind constant learning is that it makes you capable of solving many problems and adding value to people's lives. For instance, if you acquire the skills of marketing and creative writing, you become valuable for different brands who want to reach out to their target buyers. So, you need to focus on becoming a problem solver and you'll be valued over others and paid higher. On that note, think about what makes you happy and drives you to get up in the morning; pour your heart and soul into it.

Most people live frustrated because they don't make efforts toward improving their financial literacy. Even though they hate their paycheck-to-paycheck cycle, they still choose to live with it. Why? Because they find it too overwhelming to make a change and do something new. They continue to give a significant portion of their earnings to the government in the form of taxes. The higher the paycheck, the higher the taxes you need to pay. However, if you choose to educate yourself about making money from different sources and retaining most of your income, you can walk on the path of financial freedom.

It's better to work a little harder now and get out of your comfort zone than to stay in a job all your life and still have no idea about your finances. You should consider taking up a side hustle or creating a medium of passive income to boost your earnings.

Visualize and Believe

The journey of amassing wealth has to begin with faith. If you don't first believe what you want to achieve, you will never get to the point of working toward it convincingly. Success is all about doing. If you don't take action, you remain where you are. After you believe, you need to visualize it. The moment you imagine something that doesn't exist as if it does, your mind begins to function toward acquiring it.

People who're able to attain wealth have positive mindsets. They begin their journey of building wealth in their thoughts first. It's their desire to have a certain lifestyle, own a high-end car and a big house, be able to provide for their family, and support a charity of their choice that determines how much they're supposed to earn to be able to fulfill all of that.

You shouldn't be vague in your approach to building wealth. You should know how much you need to earn because that sets you on the path of being serious about your goals.

Plan and Take Action

A desire is futile unless it's turned into an action, which is possible only with organized planning. You need to structure your thoughts and know how you want to achieve your goals. There has to be a step-by-step process that you need to think about before taking any action. So, when it comes to making money, you need to ensure that you do the right thing. Perhaps you need to read personal finance books, talk to experts, and also try to spend more time with people who have good financial knowledge. In order to ensure that your plan succeeds, you need to take sound advice. While there are certain things you need to execute yourself, you should seek support from people who're more experienced than you.

As discussed in the previous chapter, budgeting is the foundation of financial planning. People who're spendthrifts find budgeting scary because it makes them feel like it's a punishment. But that's not true at all. Budgeting simply means planning your spending. You don't need to stay away from watching movies or going out, but you need to plan these things ahead of time. There's a difference between spending whenever you feel like without a plan and having a spending plan. When you have a definite spending plan, you always know where your money is going. You're not surprised or shocked when you review your bank statements.

When you have a spending plan, you always have money to pay your bills and meet all the necessary expenses. In addition, you're also able to pay for anything that comes up unexpectedly, such as a medical expense or a new outfit for an event.

To make a spending plan, you need to know your income and expenditure each month. Besides the usual monthly expenses, you need to separate a part of your income for emergencies and other important things like car repair, insurance, or family holidays.

Your spending plan is effective if it helps you pay your bills on time, keeps you from buying anything impulsively, and boosts your savings. The biggest change a good spending plan can bring is that you won't be stressed about money.

Build and Sustain Wealth

Getting rich is perhaps easier than staying rich. When you try to increase your income, save, and make various financial investments, you feel excited about it all. The challenging part is to keep the earned wealth. Most people falter when they have enough because they don't know how to preserve their money and make it grow. There are so many people who make millions and billions, but they end up losing all their wealth to mindless spendings, taxes, and lawsuits. So, learning to handle money well is as important as making an income.

Those who know how to sustain their wealth are able to multiply even their little savings. The key to staying rich is practicing caution when it comes to spending and keeping the future in mind. You should keep in mind that just because you're rich doesn't mean you can spend as much as you want. You still need to ensure that you don't go beyond your means. Also, you need to understand that times are never the same. The things that worked in your favor in the past might not help you today.

You should keep the following tactics in mind to protect your riches:

- Be consistent in your savings and investments. Never stop putting money into different saving and investment instruments (stocks, bonds, cash, and commodities). Remember, the compounding effect in the growth of your money is dependent on market conditions.

- Be prepared for unpredictable circumstances. Your financial planning should include building sufficient funds for medical emergencies and unexpected scenarios like income loss.

- Be cautious and confident at the same time. While it's good to be optimistic and expect a good return over the long haul, you should also be realistic.

- Keep an eye on your checking account and ensure there are no fraudulent activities or unauthorized charges. You must also check for all kinds of banking fees, such as late fees, overdraft fees, maintenance fees, and ATM fees. Monitoring your checking account periodically can also help you stay on track with your expenses.

Being financially educated begins with knowing your potential to the fullest and utilizing it well to be able to maximize your earnings and scope for growth. You need to believe in your ability to create wealth and visualize your financial freedom to be able to achieve it. Then you need to carve out a realistic plan and begin taking consistent action. Also, before you even accumulate plenty of money, you should know how to preserve it.

Now the next step is to understand the importance of investing, which we're going to learn in the next chapter.

Chapter 3: Importance of Investing

"Make every dollar work for you." –Unknown

So, why should you invest? Isn't saving enough? It's perhaps the most relevant question to ask yourself today, considering the pace at which the prices of goods and services are rising, eroding the value of money. While saving protects your hard-earned money, it doesn't really help you become wealthy. You put aside some money in a savings account and leave it untouched, so that you can dip into it on a rainy day. Savings can also help you meet some of your short-term goals. However, when you invest your money, meaning you put it in growth instruments like stocks, mutual funds, ETFs, and bonds, you allow it to multiply exponentially over time. There's actually no limit to how much you can make your money grow, as long as you stay invested and never quit. Those who invest their money are able to replace human capital with financial capital, which sets them free from the traditional workforce. With more money at hand, they can get rid of all their debts and liabilities earlier in life and fulfill all their dreams sooner.

So, if you haven't started investing yet, you need to understand what's keeping you from putting your money to work. Is it fear of losing money? Are you waiting for a higher paycheck or is it pure procrastination? Whatever it is, just shrug it off and get started! There's no right moment to begin investing. You don't have to wait for the markets to recover or till you get a better job. Be aware that the economy is never going to be the same. It's bound to undergo many ups and downs. An investor needs to focus on the long-term growth of the market, which is more likely to be positive. Yes, there are risks and rewards of investing, which you need to keep in mind before choosing an investment asset. You certainly do need a strategic approach to the whole ball game of investing, which is staying invested for a long period of time and putting your money in a variety of asset classes.

The best part about investing is that you can start even with a small amount and keep building upon it. You don't have to have huge sums of money to be successful at investing.

Scope for Long-Term Returns

If you're patient with your money, it has the potential to give you good returns over the long haul. You need to have the right mindset for it and learn to manage your emotions. People who look for instant profits often bet on highly risky stocks without any knowledge and understanding of the market, which leads to loss. You don't have to do that. Never treat investing like gambling. Instead, go for the safer path and aim at long-term returns. When you invest in a consistent and disciplined manner, you get the advantage of dollar-cost averaging, which reduces your average price per share and safeguards your investments against market volatility.

Whether you buy an individual stock or real estate, you need to keep the long-term profit in mind and stay committed to it. In addition, you can also expect to earn dividends from your stocks and rental income from the property you own.

Helping to Surpass Inflation

Whether you like it or not, the prices of everything you need to buy are always going to increase over time. The fact that money loses its buying power every decade indicates that you need to find ways to generate more money to be able to afford everything you need or want 10 years down the road. You may or may not get a raise in your salary, but the costs of goods and services are definitely going to go up. So, the best way to outdo inflation is to put your money to work. You can expect to receive significant capital growth if you invest in appreciating assets.

Source of Extra Income

Financial investments also work like an additional income, which we all need. If you invest regularly, you'll not just witness a continued increase in your wealth, but also your passive income. You may want to withdraw the profit earned through your investments to use it for your daily living expenses, or you can reinvest it for further growth. It can be a perfect regular income plan for retirees and also for those who want to take a career break and explore new avenues.

You can earn income in the form of dividends, which is a portion of the profits made by the company, from investments like stocks, bonds, and ETFs. Since there are several companies that announce dividend payouts on a monthly, quarterly, or annual basis, you can treat it like a passive income.

Higher Investment Returns

You can expect to receive higher returns from stocks compared to options like commodities, certificates of deposit, and treasury bonds. If we look at history, the average return given by the stock market in the last 90 years has been around 10% annually. On the other hand, if we consider the returns given by long-term government bonds, it's been approximately 5% to 6% annually during the time horizon (DiLallo, 2020).

Although you have to keep your money blocked for a long period of time (maybe a decade or two), you can look forward to higher yields eventually. For instance, when you buy a property at a certain price today, you need to wait for its value to increase over time. You might have to give away a large part of your earnings and savings initially, but you get a much higher return when you sell it off after some years.

Accomplish Key Financial Goals

Whether you want to pay off your student loan, buy a new car, build up cash for a house downpayment, or retire by a certain age, your investments can help you achieve all your important financial goals much faster than any other saving instruments can ever do. The secret to living your desired life isn't really chasing a paycheck that barely pays your bills. While it's good to have a day job and take up a side hustle or two (we'll learn about this in Chapter 8) to meet all your needs, it's investing in a planned and consistent manner that gives you the opportunity to enjoy a financially secure life.

However, you need to be careful about how you approach investing. If you buy any random stock just because somebody else made lots of money out of it, you're more likely to go backward in your financial roadmap than make any progress. The decisions you make in regard to where you want to invest has to be yours and it should align with your life vision.

Remember, the journey of becoming wealthy has to be slow and steady. Investing is for everybody, irrespective of the size of an individual's income. Those who begin investing early in life are able to see the compounding power of growth in their funds. The reward for never quitting is the interest you earn

　　　　　　　　　　　　　　E. A. SPARKS

on already earned interest and your principal amount, which turns out to be a huge amount over the period of 10 or 20 years.

So, how should you decide where to invest? In the next chapter, we're going to learn about various investment options and their significance.

Chapter 4: Types of Investments

"There is no more profitable investment than investing in yourself." –Roy T. Bennett

The more you work on yourself and harness the power of your skills, expertise, and knowledge, the higher the income you can generate. An investment of any kind requires you to put in work consistently to be able to produce something valuable out of it. The first thing you need to understand about investments is that it's all about time and patience. You need to wait to see the profitable outcome. Also, there's no investment devoid of risks. If you have chances of gains, there are possibilities of losses, too. Hence, you need to be tactful about investing.

In order to make maximum profits and avoid losing money, you need to understand the basic concepts of investing. To begin with, you need to stay unaffected by the highs and lows of the market because your ultimate returns depend on the overall market performance. There will be phases when most stocks will decline in value and if you're invested in any of them, you'll also lose some money. However, the very same stocks can rise up in value and enable you to earn a return on your investment. So, the tactic is to believe in your investment and stay with it. The longer you stay in an investment, the better the return you're likely to secure.

The asset classes available to you to invest in can open new doors of making high returns. However, you need to pick what makes sense to you personally and not necessarily what seems to be popular. While diversification is an integral aspect of investing, you should refrain from putting your money just about everywhere without knowledge. Typically, not all asset classes make profits or undergo losses at the same time; for instance, when stocks fall, real estate usually does well. Inflation is good news for investors who want to sell off their properties, as they're likely to get higher value on their investments. Similarly, when prices of commodities like gold and silver appreciate in value, bonds may be an undesirable asset class to invest in.

So, of course, you need to diversify your investments. It's never wise to rely on any one particular asset class. Since you can't predict which sectors and industries are going to perform well in the future, you need to distribute your money allocations in multiple stocks to increase your probability of profits.

Let's look at the types of investments you can make:

Stocks

Perhaps one of the most popular mediums to invest your money, but not very well understood by most investors, is stock market investment. Some people stay away from it, thinking it's too risky, while others end up betting most of their income without gaining much understanding. However, if you understand it correctly and invest wisely, buying stocks and being able to sell them at higher prices later is an excellent way to earn profits.

When you buy a stock, you actually acquire a small ownership in the company. Thus, you're supposed to choose your stock with the utmost care. It's like investing in somebody else's business. You won't invest in a business if you don't like their ideas and the way they operate, right? Similarly, when you put your money in an individual stock, you need to like the company and their products. If you think a particular company makes good products and their value is going to rise, you may want to invest in it. When a company's stock prices increase, investors make money and vice versa.

If you have surplus funds to invest and can afford to take risk, a large part of your portfolio can have stocks. However, if you have debts and liabilities to pay, you should avoid stock market investment or put in only a small amount of money.

Bonds

Investing in bonds can be a great way of keeping your portfolio diversified and able to deal with the stock market's volatility. Bonds are debt instruments; they're loans taken out by companies, municipalities, and governments for various projects. In this scenario, the creditor is the investor who lends a certain amount of money to the concerned entity. So, you make money when the borrower returns the money with interest after a period of time. Although bonds typically pay a fixed rate of interest to debtholders, you can also expect to receive variable interest rates these days.

You must take into account if the tenure of the bond is aligned to the time horizon you've set to reach your goals. There are short-term bonds that take one to three years to mature; then there are mid-term bonds that mature in more than 10 years. Long-term bonds mature somewhere between 10 to 30 years.

Those with low risk tolerance can allocate a higher percentage of their funds in bonds, as they're known to be safer investments in comparison to stocks. Nevertheless, investors should be aware that bond issuers can default and they may not be in a position to pay back the debt on time. Besides, if there's a rise in interest rates, the bond prices may decline and investors may not benefit much.

Options

While you may not want to consider options trading as an investment option in the beginning of your investing journey, it can be a great way to diversify your portfolio and enjoy some flexibility. To put it in simple terms, options trading is a kind of a deal that allows you (the buyer) the "option" to buy or sell an underlying asset, which could be a specific security at a predetermined price within a certain time period. The security can be held for a day or for even up to two years. However, the buyer is not obligated to make the purchase.

You don't need a huge amount to invest in options. In fact, it's better to put in only a small sum of money and play it safe. You may feel tempted to speculate stock price movements; however, it's highly risky and most investors fail at it and bear heavy losses. Hence, you should keep your life goals in mind and invest cautiously.

Mutual Funds and ETFs

If you don't want to take the pain of studying the individual stocks and keeping an eye on the market, mutual funds and ETFs (Exchange Traded Funds) are your best bet. Both mutual funds and ETFs comprise a bunch of different assets and securities, which allows you to have a good mix of different sectors and industries in your portfolio. Thus, you get an automatic diversification. While both are handled by fund managers, they're dissimilar in their trading style. ETFs are purchased and sold like stocks; hence, their prices fluctuate throughout the day. On the other hand, mutual funds are traded at the end of each business day.

Both mutual funds and ETFs are beneficial, as they help you generate stable returns in the long run, which is ideal for retirement planning. However, if you prefer liquidity of a stock, you may want to pick an ETF.

You should keep in mind that investing in mutual funds and ETFs comes with a few minor costs, which may impact your overall returns. Thus, you should try to choose the funds that have the lowest fees and charges.

Real Estate

While real estate may not be the easiest asset class to own, it can be one of the best ways to increase your net worth. Besides helping you diversify your portfolio, real estate also makes your risk-return profile stronger by offering lower chances of losses. If you compare it to stocks and bonds, real estate is less volatile, too. Not to mention the returns you can expect from a property, land, or a house can be way higher than any other investments can ever offer. The best part is that you don't need to have all the cash available to make an outright purchase. You can own a property, even with borrowed money, and still have an asset that has the potential to appreciate in value over time.

Cryptocurrency and Non-Fungible Tokens (NFT)

Cryptocurrencies and NFTs are new-age investments that promise to pay you exceptionally high returns and help you outpace inflation. Of course, the risks are high too. So, you need to be careful about how you want to go about investing in such highly volatile assets. There's a whole chapter dedicated to these assets ahead in the book, which should give you an insight into their mechanisms.

Whether it's a good idea to invest in cryptocurrencies or not is a matter of supply and demand. Cryptocurrencies are digital currencies (Bitcoin, Ethereum, Tether, and others) that gain their value when more and more people want to own them. So, the more retail and institutional investors buy cryptocurrencies, the better chances you have of drawing profits from your investment.

NFTs are digital assets, backed by blockchain technology, that have their own distinctive identification codes and metadata that sets each of them apart. The value of these cryptographic assets is derived from their exclusivity. While cryptocurrencies are identical and can be traded, non-fungible tokens cannot be replicated. The purpose of NFTs is to represent physical assets like artwork and real estate in a digital format to its buyers. They're meant to eliminate intermediaries and make transactions simpler. Thus, they make up a whole new market for investors to explore.

Owning a Business

When you own a business, you have the potential of making unlimited money. While you may not have the stability and security of a fixed paycheck each month, a business can give you flexibility, freedom, and varied growth opportunities. Thus, it can be one of the best financial investments you can ever make. But, of course, there are risks involved, and failures are not rare. Many businesses do not survive more than five years due to various reasons. However, the majority of business owners are happy with their decision of starting something of their own. It has not just helped them attain financial freedom, but also allowed them to live life on their own terms.

So, you can pick and choose the investment vehicle that best suits your life goals and preferences. While it's good to distribute money in different asset classes to minimize chances of losses, it's not wise to diversify your portfolio excessively. Also, you should never invest in something that's too complicated for you to understand. Spend time growing your financial knowledge and keep a modest approach to investing to be able to achieve stable returns.

Let's get to learning about the stock market and how to invest in it to make money in the next chapter.

Chapter 5: Stock Market

"The stock market is filled with individuals who know the price of everything, but the value of nothing." –Phillip Fisher

The most fascinating part about investing in the stock market is becoming part of a business and owning its value. It's a kind of passive style of entrepreneurship, where you don't have to take the responsibilities of creating a business plan and executing it; however, you have a share in the profits and losses. Buying a share of a company simply means acquiring a piece of ownership. So, if you really like a product and believe it's valuable, you can choose to buy its shares in anticipation that its stock prices will rise. The key to making money in the stock market is to buy a stock at a low price and sell it off later at an increased price. However, nobody can control or predict that. When a company's share prices decline, the value of its stocks also decrease and investors lose money; however, when the same stock performs well, meaning more and more investors buy its shares, the prices go up and everybody makes money.

The stock market allows you to grow your wealth in a magnificent manner. Nevertheless, if you don't practice caution, you may also lose money miserably.

The rule of thumb to any kind of risky investment is that you should never utilize funds that you've separated to fulfill an important life milestone, such as your child's higher education, house downpayment, or retirement. You should either have a windfall of money or surplus savings for investment purposes. That said, it's not necessary to invest a large sum of money, especially while you're still quite new and inexperienced as an investor. You need to keep in mind that stock market investment is a long-term deal that you need to stick with to reap significant returns. You need to understand that stocks by nature are highly volatile. They aren't meant to stay stable. Thus, you can't be sure of your profits. The investors who get greedy and invest a lot of money in one go often suffer a downfall. The safer approach is to put in small amounts of money on a consistent basis.

Choose Your Investing Style

There are different ways to invest in the stock market. Some people, who're new to investing, choose to take help from financial experts, who invest their money in suitable stocks. Typically, brokerage firms or independent financial advisors try to pick stocks or funds according to your goals. However, if they simply take your money and invest without talking to you about why you'd like to invest and a little bit about your life vision, you should refrain from taking their guidance. As an investor, you should make an informed investment decision and have clarity about your objective behind it.

Another way people invest is through their employer's 401(k), which enables them to get access to some of the stock mutual funds. However, they don't get to choose individual stocks. It's a simple practice of making regular contributions every month for long-term growth in your funds.

Then, there are investors who prefer to pick stocks of their choice. They have absolute clarity about what they want to achieve in the long run and they aren't affected by what's happening in the economy. They simply invest based on their knowledge and understanding.

No matter which way you want to go, the main idea is to invest prudently and never get carried away by your emotions.

Brokerage Account or Robo-Advisor

The next thing to decide is whether you want to open a brokerage account and invest manually or you want to do it via a robo-advisor. The difference between the two types of accounts is in the way they operate—a brokerage account allows you to make multiple types of investments, such as stocks, bonds, ETFs, mutual funds, and have all kinds of retirement accounts (IRAs, 401(k), and others), while a robo-advisor is an automated investing service that manages your investments on your behalf. Both processes take very little time to start and charge a minimal fee.

You can have more than one brokerage account and deposit as much money as you like. However, you don't need to pay any fee to open an account. It's only when you want to make a purchase (make an investment), you'll have to fund your account with the required money. Your brokerage account is the mediator between you and the investment you want to make.

A robo-advisor can help you with different things related to your investments like rebalancing your portfolio to optimizing tax savings without any human interaction. You'll need to share your investing objectives in order for the advisor to establish your portfolio. While you may have to pay a commission to buy or sell investments in a brokerage account, you won't usually pay any such fees with a robo-advisor.

Also, the majority of robo-advisors can handle both individual retirement accounts and taxable accounts for you. While some robo-advisors require you to invest at least $5,000 or higher, a majority of them have a minimum requirement of $500 or lower.

So, you can go for a brokerage account if you'd like to take care of investments by yourself. However, if you don't have the time or the inclination to manage it independently, you can choose a robo-advisor.

Individual Stocks and Mutual Funds Are Two Different Investment Methods

While investing in mutual funds is also a kind of stock market investing, it's different from buying individual stocks. When you invest in an ETF, index fund, or an equity mutual fund, you purchase multiple stocks of multiple companies; however, when you invest in a stock, it's only for a particular company. ETFs and Index funds simply monitor an index, meaning if you've bought a Standard & Poor's 500 fund or a Nasdaq 100, it's going to mirror the holdings of whatever index they monitor. Since you get to be a part of several companies of different industries, your portfolio is automatically diversified and your risk of losing money also reduces.

If you want to purchase individual stocks, you'll have to get into deeper research and understanding of various sectors and industries before you settle on a company's stock to invest in. It's riskier in comparison to mutual funds because you're betting on only one company and market conditions are never static. Nonetheless, you can diversify your investment by picking stocks of multiple companies. But, of course, you'll have to devote more time in studying about various companies.

Investing in mutual funds can be beneficial in terms of building a reasonably handsome nest egg for retirement. You should not expect great returns in the short-term, let's say a year or two. It's clearly a game of patience because you need to keep investing regularly for a really long period of time to build wealth. On the other hand, you can witness a significant jump in your investment in stocks even in a short period of time. However, you're also quite likely to lose your invested amount if your chosen stock performs poorly. So, you need to be sure about the kind of stocks you choose for investments.

Create a Budget for Stock Investments

Many people stay away from stock investing assuming it's expensive and out of reach for them. However, that's far from the truth. It can be as costly or as budget-friendly as you'd like it to be. The basic idea to keep in mind is that you should never get reckless with your investments. As long as you're cautious and understand what you're getting into, you can secure value for every penny that you put in. As stated earlier in the chapter, you don't need to start with a big amount. Even if you invest $500 a month, it can become huge over time.

If you think you don't have enough money to be able to invest, you may have to reevaluate your monthly budget, and also review areas like how much debt you owe, your income level, and your future plans. If you have multiple debts of high amounts, you should make efforts to pay them off on priority or at least try to minimize them. As far as your earnings and expenses are concerned, you need to deal with your discretionary spendings, such as takeout coffee, movies, clubbing, and shopping. You can perhaps cut down on each of them a little bit every month and allocate the savings toward investing in a mutual fund. It can be a small amount.

When you think about how you'd like to live a decade from now, it can be much easier to feel motivated to shell out money to invest. Most people are never able to start their investing journey because they don't prioritize it. They always think about it after they've spent most of their earnings on all kinds of needs and wants. Keeping a certain amount of money for investments should be part of your budget planning. If you do it deliberately, you'll automatically get into the habit of investing and you'll never regret it.

Target Long-Term Investing

When you think of investing, think long-term. There's nothing like short-term gains unless you want to try day trading, which is a totally different ball game for totally different investors. However, the smarter approach to stock market investing is to buy the stocks of companies that you think are good and take the long route of holding your investments. People who simply stay invested for a horizon of 10–15 years or longer are able to surpass the ups and downs of the market. If you expect great returns within a time-span of six months or a year, you're more likely to bear the impact of the changing market conditions.

If we consider the history of the US stock market, we see that those who refrained from selling their S&P 500 investments for 10 years were able to rake in an average profit of 13% ("Which Investments Have the Highest Historical Returns?", 2022). Statistics prove that keeping a long time horizon of investments protects you from sharp market declines and losses.

The best part about holding investments for the long-term is that you don't have to get into the technical analysis of different stocks. You can simply be patient and lay out a simple roadmap to maximize your gains.

Here's what you can do:

- Pick small companies that are fairly new but have lots of growth potential. The benefit of buying their stocks is that you can expect to gain capital appreciation in the long run when such companies expand their businesses and their share prices increase.

- Look for undervalued companies, meaning stocks that are being sold for less than their intrinsic value. There are times when stock markets reduce or increase prices of certain stocks based on the media buzz about a company irrespective of its fundamentals. So, you as an investor should look for the real value of a company and consider buying its stock when their prices are on a decline.

- Opt for companies that pay their shareholders regular cash dividends. It can prove to be a clever long-term strategy, as the dividend-paying companies do pay out at least the partial return on investment. Also, the majority of such companies increase their dividend amounts with time. Not to mention that the returns that you can expect to receive from a dividend yield can be way higher than government bonds.

Evaluate Your Portfolio Periodically

Although a long-term investing approach doesn't require much of an investor's intervention in terms of checking the performance of stocks, you do need to make sure that your portfolio is well-balanced. You need to take a look at your investments from time to time to check if they're aligned to your financial goals and the time horizon you have in mind to reach them. For instance, if you think the fluctuating market conditions have hit your investments, you need to perhaps rebalance your portfolio by reallocating a higher percentage of money toward fixed-income investments. In another scenario, if your allocations are perfect and your stocks are doing fine, you can consider adding more investments to your portfolio.

You should also ensure that you have stocks or funds from a variety of industries and sectors. If you see that you've put in lots of money in a technology fund, maybe you can direct some of it toward other promising sectors like aviation, infrastructure, or healthcare. Besides, you should upgrade your portfolio by adding some of the international stocks that you think might make money in the long run.

Being aware of the fees, charges, and taxes is also part of managing your investments. So, whenever you pick a mutual fund or an individual stock, make sure you aren't giving away a large part of your ultimate earnings to fund managers and brokers. You should look for lower expense ratio fees and commissions.

Then, the biggest hurdle to tackle in the way of maximizing your returns are taxes. Yes, you do need to pay taxes on your capital gains; however, you can minimize its implications by applying certain strategies:

- Pick tax-efficient funds like index funds and ETFs.

- Keep your tax-efficient assets (index mutual funds, ETFs, bonds, and stocks) in taxable accounts and less tax-efficient assets (taxable bonds and actively managed mutual funds) in nontaxable accounts.

- Hold your investments longer to save on taxes. If you sell off your investments within a year, you're liable to pay taxes just as you pay for a regular income; however, you can cut down on taxes automatically on your long-term capital gains.

Stock market investments are risky because of the volatility of the stock prices. Thus, you need to invest in a cautious manner and try to minimize losses. Whether you choose to buy individual stocks or invest in mutual funds, keep the long-term perspective and build a diversified portfolio to reap maximum profits.

In the next chapter, we'll learn about one of the most valuable asset classes that all kinds of investors should consider making part of their portfolios.

Chapter 6: Real Estate

"Real estate is the purest form of entrepreneurship" –Brian Buffini

There's no investment quite like real estate. If you manage to buy a property, you have plenty of ways to amplify your wealth. You don't just get a chance to create a stable income source by renting out your property, but you can also wait for its value to increase and sell it off at a higher price. Real estate is also an effective diversification strategy for investors, as it can minimize their portfolio volatility by keeping a lower correlation with other key asset classes. However, the biggest benefit of owning real estate is that it helps you beat inflation. The rate at which the value of your property appreciates is typically higher than the rate of rising consumer prices, which means you're likely to secure handsome capital gains eventually. High inflation isn't grim news for real estate owners because it can help them charge higher rental fees from their tenants.

Investors also have access to using leverage in case they don't have enough funds to afford a property. They can pay a small part of the total cost up front and continue to pay the remaining money over time. So, you get to own the entire property and still maintain your savings.

That said, owning real estate does come with a few challenges. The fact that real estate prices are at their peak means that buying a house can be a highly expensive investment. Besides, there are quite a few hassles associated with being a property-owner, such as dealing with repair work, renovations, and paying property taxes. Not to mention you need to pay high mortgage fees for the life of the loan unless you want to make an outright purchase, which isn't possible for the majority of investors.

While all of the above is true about real estate investing, the possibility of making huge profits in the long run can't be denied either. So, let's look into different ways you can get started in your real estate investing journey:

Rental Properties

Apart from making money by selling a property when its value has appreciated, real estate owners can have regular flow of cash by renting it out. It's one of the best modes of generating a side income, which is passive in nature. You don't have to wait to rent out your property until you've paid off the entire mortgage, but you can begin earning the rental income right away. So, in a way, your tenant can help reduce your loan burden, and once it's completely paid off, you can take home all the earnings. Additionally, there are quite a few tax benefits of renting your property, like the ability to claim deductions for expenses like repair and operating costs, meaning you get a chance to cut down on your mortgage interest and insurance fees.

While there are many potential advantages to renting out your property, you should be willing to deal with multiple issues related to being a landlord, such as dealing with tenants, maintaining the property, and paying all kinds of fees (HOA, homeowners insurance, taxes, and others). Besides, you need to be okay with not making an income when your property is vacant. As long as you're ready for all that goes into buying a property and have calculated an estimate of your profits by renting it, you should go for it. You shouldn't just buy a property and then feel overwhelmed by everything that might unfold. You also need to be aware that the housing sector isn't the most stable market; there are factors like supply and demand, location, and the economy that determine a property's value.

Before you get into the rental property business, you need to ensure that your returns are greater than other modest investments like dividend-paying stocks and government securities considering the risks involved.

Below is a basic guideline to buying a rental property. Keep in mind that you need to focus on maximizing your returns and try to minimize potential losses:

- The first step should be to calculate the possible return on investment (ROI) of the property you'd like to purchase. In order to do that, you need to draw an estimate of the yearly rental income of the property. If there's pet rent applicable, include that as well. Then, calculate all the yearly expenses related to managing the property. Finally, deduct the total expenses from total earnings, which is possibly your actual earnings. Don't forget to take into account the down payment and upfront expenses. From there, divide yearly earnings by the total money invested.

- You should make sure that the area where the property is located has a growing population and enough job prospects for people to want to live there.

- You need to check the percentage of households who live in rental apartments/houses in the area.

- You should also check if the rental prices are on a rise and if the vacancy rates are decreasing.

- If it's your first real estate investment, try to find a property, which is rent-ready or already has a tenant, as it can reduce risk significantly.

- You should look for a city and state with low property tax rates, so that it lessens your overall investment costs.

- The locality should have all the preferred amenities like easy access to public transport, schools, coffee shops, restaurants, shopping malls, and public parks.

- Do your research and understand the real estate market. You may also want to talk to property agents and investors who've had the experience of buying rental properties.

You can succeed at making rental properties a wealth creating machine with the right understanding of the costs involved, forecasting the ROIs, and researching the market.

REITS (Real Estate Investment Trusts)

Buying a property can be one of the best investment decisions for anyone; however, not everyone has the bandwidth for it, especially in terms of finances. So, those who find it too intimidating to even make the down payment for a property can choose to invest in REITs. In doing so, you are owning real estate without actually buying a physical property.

REITs are companies that own commercial properties like hotels, malls, offices, healthcare facilities, and warehouses. You can become a fractional owner of several commercial properties without buying them and worrying about their management costs. Besides, you can also invest in residential properties, which are known as residential REITs. So, you don't need to take the headache of paying mortgage fees every month and maintaining the property like you do with a traditional real estate investment. The best part is that unlike physical properties, REITs are liquid assets, which can be traded quite quickly as per your choice.

Since REITs are bought and sold on exchanges, you can invest in them just like you'd pick stocks or funds. On that note, if the value of the properties you've invested in goes up, you make money. There are two ways that shareholders receive value for their investment:

- Dividend payout
- Property value appreciation

While the value of REITs can dwindle, the reliable source of income is the rents for commercial properties. The tenants are typically bound by long-term leases. Also, when the properties are financed, they generate interest payments.

So, investors can expect to earn a decent amount of money with the increase in the property occupancy rates and rental prices.

Considering the long-term gains that REITs can bring, it's one of the most prudent ways to deal with the rising inflation rate. On top of that, it can help you diversify your investments because of its relatively lower volatility.

House Flipping

When you buy a property at a low price and are able to sell it off at a high price within a short span of time, preferably within a year or even months, it's called house flipping. At the same time, some investors simply purchase a house and wait for its value to appreciate, which is called the buy-and-hold approach. However, real house flipping is about buying an undervalued house and making it market-ready. A property can be low-priced for several reasons, as its owners could potentially be in financial distress and unable to manage it anymore, or it's in a structurally bad shape.

If you'd like to dabble in property flipping, you should adhere to the points mentioned below:

- You should know how much you can really spend before venturing into the flipping business. The costs of repair and renovation can be high and if you end up spending quite a lot and aren't able to sell it off quickly, it's not going to be profitable.

- Follow the 70% rule when you decide to pay for a property, which says that you should not pay more than 70% of your after-repair value (ARV) after subtracting repair and renovation costs.

- Spend time researching and taking guidance from a real estate agent, who will know a great deal about price-growth projections.

- Get the right kind of contractors on board for repair work. Check their licenses and rates. Make sure you get a perfect job done within your budget.

- Choose to work with only experienced and esteemed professionals for handling taxes, promoting your property, and taking advice regarding property flipping. Remember, you need to treat it like a business to get a high return on your investment.

Flipping properties can be a highly profitable undertaking as long as you play it right, meaning you pick the right property, which is possible only when you know the market really well. It really doesn't make much economic sense to take out a loan to buy a dilapidated property, pay taxes, and bear the renovation costs. However, if you're an experienced investor and have enough cash available, you can turn it into a full-fledged business.

Online Real Estate Platforms and Crowdfunding

Another different and potentially simpler way of investing in real estate, apart from REITs, is real estate crowdfunding. This is a method for connecting investors with companies who want to raise capital to be able to invest in real estate. It's an opportunity for investors who do not have the capital for real estate investment, but they want to take advantage of the growth potential of the real estate market.

Investors and companies can connect on crowdfunding portals and social media sites like Facebook, LinkedIn, and Twitter. When multiple people contribute their bit, a large sum of money can be collected and invested in real estate. So, it's a win-win for both investors and companies who actually make the investments. As an investor, you get a chance to participate passively in a huge investment, which can generate huge returns for you in the long run. It's an easy alternative to buying a physical property and dealing with all sorts of legalities and costs.

While it's a clever investment, you need to be wary of certain risks, as you can't always trust the companies you want to give your money to. They don't have solid financial track records to prove their performance. Hence, investors do have the probability of losing their invested funds. That being said, you can still give it a try after doing your due diligence and ensuring that the team behind the investment is genuine.

Airbnb

You can also break away from the traditional idea of real estate investing by buying a property from a short-term rental perspective. Instead of going the buy-and-hold path or getting into rental properties and the ball game of looking for tenants, you can consider running an Airbnb business, which can be a lot more profitable. The basic approach to vacation rental investment is finding a property which is likely to attract travelers. If you purchase an Airbnb property in a city or area that nobody wants to visit, your investment is likely to fail. So, location is key when it comes to Airbnb homes. You need to think like a tourist while picking a property, meaning it has to be close to all the main city attractions, and not very far from the airport and public transport.

Then, the next crucial part to be sure of is the local laws and regulations of the city you want to buy your short-term rental in. Remember, the rules of running an Airbnb business are different in different states. There are cities where you're not allowed to establish a short-term rental business.

So, after you've decided on a property, all you need to do is arrange for a mortgage and get ready to set up the place for Airbnb hosting. There are overhead and ongoing costs of running an Airbnb business, and if you want to hire a management staff to take care of the operational tasks on your behalf, you'll be paying them as well. As well, you'll also be shelling out money on property maintenance and taxes. However, there are many tax deductions that you can claim as the owner of a short-term vacation rental.

The key to maximizing your profits is pricing your rental right and keeping the occupancy rate high. You need to be strategic about running a business. No matter how beautiful your property is or how nicely you treat your guests, your business will flourish and prove sustainable only when you know how to maintain consistent cash flow. While you can make a lot more money than a regular rental property owner would earn in a month, you should be ready to handle dips in guest reservations during low seasons. So, you need to manage pricing based on the current market demand.

Besides, you should aim to grow your short-term rental business by owning multiple properties. If you don't have the time to do it yourself, you can hire Airbnb hosts and property managers across properties. Of course, you'll need to choose people who have a similar vision to yours and are able to execute things passionately. The bottom-line is that an Airbnb business can be run in different ways. You can be the property owner and the host, or you can choose to hire people for different jobs. The main purpose is to convert it into a profit-making business in a creative way.

Real estate investing in any form is a sensible approach to building wealth. Keep in mind, though, that it requires knowledge, understanding of the market, and patience. However, it pays off well in the end as long as you know what you've gotten yourself into.

In the next chapter, we'll learn about one of the most innovative mediums of investing.

Chapter 7: Cryptocurrency and Non-Fungible Tokens (NFTs)

"If you don't believe it or don't get it, I don't have the time to try to convince you, sorry." –Satoshi Nakamoto

As an investor, you have a whole gamut of options to explore to be able to create possibilities of making more money. So, yes, you shouldn't shy away from dabbling in cryptocurrencies and non-fungible tokens (NFTs). They may sound scary or unrelatable to a novice investor, but anything that has value can make you rich if you invest in it. To begin with, both cryptocurrencies and NFTs are highly volatile in terms of their demand; thus, these are highly risky investments.

Cryptocurrency is digital money. Powered by blockchain technology, it's a purely decentralized method of currency exchange, meaning it isn't controlled by any government or central authority and it requires no bank to validate transactions. So, if you want to pay somebody via cryptocurrency, it's going to be recorded in a public ledger, and your virtual money (cryptocurrency)

is going to be stored in a digital wallet. While there are over 19,000 cryptocurrencies, most investors prefer to bet on Bitcoin and Ethereum.

You can actually make a purchase with a cryptocurrency; however, it's typically known as an asset class, which can make you rich. Yes, people have managed to grow their money with cryptocurrency investments. It's a relatively new idea of investing, which may or may not appeal to a regular investor. But it's definitely worth learning about and knowing if it's for you or not. Remember, each investor is unique. Thus, your choice of investment assets should be distinctive. Just like any other investment, cryptocurrencies are risky, and an investor needs to be cautious about how much they want to invest and the kind of approach they want to apply to it. There are people who have put a major chunk of their earnings in cryptocurrencies and have lost all their money, which isn't a smart way to invest.

The right way to approach cryptocurrency as an investment is to first understand how it works. The value of cryptocurrency is determined by the number of people who buy it. If it's not bought by many people, the value is going to decline. Since cryptocurrency is a fairly new concept, it's going to take some time for different industries to adapt to it. Blockchain technology can help with online voting, supply chains, identity management, software security, crowdfunding, organizing data, reducing transaction costs by simplifying payment processing, and so much more. Thus, it's an interesting field to be part of as an investor.

Investing in Cryptocurrency

So, if you're curious about cryptocurrency and want to discover if it's beneficial as an investment or not, you simply need to purchase it through a stockbroker or a cryptocurrency exchange, such as Gemini, Kraken, or Cash App. You can complete the process of getting started with your cryptocurrency investment online within a few minutes. You'll need to provide your personal identification documents and bank account details to set up your profile.

You should choose a platform that offers your desired cryptocurrency, has low fees and charges and an easy withdrawal system, and is highly secure. Then, you should fund your account to begin trading. A word of caution here: You should avoid using your credit card for a cash deposit as it can be highly expensive and also risky because a cryptocurrency's value can increase or decrease anytime and you may lose all your money.

After you've bought your preferred cryptocurrency, you need to store it safely, which is a highly critical aspect of the entire process. You can either leave it in the crypto wallet, which is attached to your exchange, or you can move it to a hot or cold wallet. A hot wallet is a digital wallet, which can be stored in online devices like phones, tablets, and laptops. While it's a convenient option, your money is at risk of being stolen while in a hot wallet. So, you may want to store it in a cold wallet, which is an offline wallet, and typically takes the form of an external device like a USB or hard drive. However, you need to make sure that your devices don't fail and that you remember the keycode to be able to access your wallet.

Picking the Right Cryptocurrency Exchange

There are so many cryptocurrency exchanges to choose from that it can get overwhelming and confusing for new investors. However, it's important to make that choice with caution because it can determine the quality of your investment experience. If you go with the wrong one, it can turn out to be a hassle and prove to be detrimental to your financial growth, meaning you could lose money. The main purpose of a cryptocurrency exchange is to connect you with other buyers and sellers, so that everybody can trade cryptocurrencies. Besides, it also allows you to store your cryptocurrencies or convert it back to real-world currency and transfer it to your bank account if you do not wish to trade.

All these exchanges display the cryptocurrencies they offer with their current market prices. Thus, it's quite simple to trade crypto via these platforms. However, you can't ignore certain grave issues like security breaches and high trading costs that are way more than what you'd pay for other assets. So, to ensure that you're able to trade safely and smoothly, you need to have a set criteria in mind:

- The first thing to be sure of is safety. You need to check if the exchange has the reputation of protecting your funds and data from potential theft and hacking. There should be protocols in place, like two-factor verification, a biometric login, a master password, and additional authentications.

• You need to pay a fee every time you trade on a cryptocurrency exchange. There are charges for trading, withdrawing, and depositing money. So, you need to check which platform has the most flexible and favorable fee structure.

• The exchange you want to trade on should have a high trading volume, meaning the sum of all buying and selling carried out within a certain time frame. It depicts the movement and direction of cryptocurrency. When the trading volume is high, you can quickly convert your cash into coins at a price that's shown to you before it changes.

• The payment method is also one of the most important factors to consider while choosing your crypto trading platform. Most exchanges allow payments via paypal, wire transfer, debit cards, credit cards, and other digital transfers. So, you need to check the fees and charges involved.

• You should also make sure that you get to pick the coins and tokens you want. Most exchanges do offer Bitcoin, the most popular of all cryptocurrencies; however, not all digital currencies are available on all platforms.

• It would be great if the exchange you choose offers an insurance policy to safeguard you against any kind of cyber crime. You should read the user agreement carefully and see what exactly is covered in the insurance.

Choosing the Cryptocurrencies to Trade

Now, to begin trading, you need to know the best valued cryptocurrencies in the market to pick and choose. You need to be aware that a single coin can have a value of thousands of dollars, which can be too expensive for new investors.

Nevertheless, you can make it affordable by purchasing just a fraction of a coin. Since cryptocurrencies like Bitcoin and Ethereum are more popular, they're priced higher than other cryptocurrencies.

Apart from demand, cryptocurrencies can rise or decline in value due to supply as well. For instance, Bitcoin is highly valued because only a certain number of Bitcoins can exist. The idea of scarcity adds to the value of the currency.

The coins you choose should have a solid use case and higher chances of being accepted by a broad section of people. For instance, Ethereum is one of the most popular coins because it can create numerous applications. So, you need to do a little bit of research on various cryptocurrencies' growth potential in the long run before investing in them.

Below are some of the best cryptocurrencies to consider for investing:

Bitcoin (BTC)

The obvious choice for a majority of investors, Bitcoin is known to be the original cryptocurrency. There are good reasons to buy Bitcoin, as it's a currency that offers the maximum liquidity and assures security. Besides, it has grown exponentially in value over the years.

Ethereum (ETH)

The second most loved cryptocurrency is Ethereum, which has also soared in value over time. Ethereum is particularly known for being a decentralized software channel that makes it possible for smart contracts and decentralized applications (dApps) to be created and run smoothly. It's supported by various global businesses, which is why investors can expect to see a huge upgrade in the days to come.

Litecoin (LTC)

Litecoin's super fast transaction processing time is said to be even better than Bitcoin. Also, Litecoin supply is going to be limited in the future; thus, it's likely to be highly valued.

Tether (USDT)

Tether can be an apprehensive investor's top choice because of its relatively lower volatility. Since it's powered by fiat money like the US dollars and the Euro, its value doesn't increase or decrease very quickly.

Cardano (ADA)

Cardano is known to be a third generation cryptocurrency with a lot of technological innovation to it. Apart from making secured and speedy transactions, you can also expect reduced energy usage.

Binance Coin (BNB)

Binance Coin has evolved from being a trade facilitator to becoming a cryptocurrency in its own right. No wonder its value has risen significantly over the years.

There are all kinds of cryptocurrencies floating around; however, you need to be careful about which you buy. As an investor, you should pick a cryptocurrency only if you understand it and believe that it has the potential to grow in value.

Storing Cryptocurrency Safely

As stated earlier, safety has to be an integral part of any cryptocurrency investment. You should be particular about how you store your cryptocurrency because if you lose it, you lose it forever. Thus, you need to store it in the safest way possible.

Custodial Wallet

A custodial wallet is the default crypto storage given to you by the trading platform. It's an arrangement where a third party stores your cryptocurrency on your behalf. The storage can be a combination of an offline storage and online storage. While it's a convenient way to both store your crypto and trade it, you need to rely on the platform's security protocols. If they go wrong, you can lose your coins. Thus, it's crucial to pick only an exchange with a heightened security system.

Cold Wallet

A cold wallet is an offline method of storing your cryptocurrency. You can keep it safely in hardware with absolutely no fear of hacking; however, it's not as convenient as online methods of storage.

Each hardware wallet comes with a recovery phrase, which helps you recover your crypto in case the device is lost or stolen. You need to keep it safe so that nobody else gets a hold of it.

Hot Wallet

A hot wallet is an online method of cryptocurrency storage, which allows you to have complete control over your cryptocurrency. You can store, send, and receive tokens via a hot wallet, which is connected to public and private keys that aid in carrying out transactions safely. Since hot wallets are an online system, they're subject to possible hacks and theft.

Investing in cryptocurrency can add a new dimension to your portfolio by opening another channel of wealth creation. However, you should never invest a huge amount of money as a new investor. The prices of digital assets can go up and down quite unpredictably. Thus, you need to watch your desired cryptocurrency closely and make a modest start. It's only when you begin to understand when to buy and sell, that you should think of betting a larger share of your money. Remember, it's not wise to lose money by making hasty decisions.

In the next chapter, we'll learn how you can maximize your savings and draw closer to your financial goals.

Chapter 8: Side Hustles

"If you are not willing to risk the usual, you will have to settle for the ordinary."
–Jim Rohn

Believe it or not, but each individual has the ability to create an additional source of income. There's no harm in making more money, right? The more you earn, the better life you can live. No two ways about it. That being said, the extra income that you draw out from a side gig doesn't have to take away every bit of your time. It shouldn't take a toll on your mental health or your relationships, either. The purpose behind a side hustle is to utilize your spare time in a much more productive way. Instead of watching TV or scrolling through your social media feed for an hour or so, you can do something valuable—and also make more money.

If you think you're too busy to take up a side job, you may want to reevaluate your daily routine and habits. A side hustle isn't supposed to add to the pressure or burden of work and responsibilities you already have. It should ideally blend into your daily schedule with ease. If it doesn't somehow, you may have to think of something else. The best part about a side gig is that you don't have to stick to it all your life. You can give it up anytime you like for whatever reason. You can dabble in it for a while and then figure out if you want to do it or not. The point being, there's lots of flexibility.

You should pick a side hustle based on your skills and interests. Don't opt for driving if you get bugged up by traffic or you hate to talk to strangers. Make sure whatever you choose goes with your personality. For instance, if you enjoy running errands, you may want to take up the job of delivering food and products to people's doorsteps. Thus, you may want to take some time to think about the things you truly enjoy and if they can be monetized.

Remember, the time and effort that you invest in a side hustle is fruitful only when the money that you generate with it goes toward your savings and aids in reaching your financial goals sooner. If you simply spend the extra money made on regular purchases, it's not going to add any value to your overall financial position.

More importantly, the money you make through a side gig acts like a shield in uncertain times. Who knew COVID-19 would happen and take away people's jobs? If you rely on only one source of income, you'll always lack the confidence to face the future. Additionally, there are tax benefits of running a side business. You can claim deductions by showing overhead and ongoing costs associated with your business at the time of tax filing.

Starting a Side Hustle

A side hustle can also be a gateway into a new career. You can make a small start and see if an idea works for you and then get into it completely. We all want to make extra money, but we are often left wondering what to do and where to start. However, it's not so hard, as long as you don't overwhelm yourself by thinking about too many things at the same time. Remember, a side gig doesn't always have to come with an initial capital investment. There are so many things that you can begin doing with zero cash on hand.

Keep the points mentioned below in mind while thinking of starting a new side hustle:

Be Aware of Your Purpose

To begin with, you should know why you want to make extra money and what motivates you to put in extra hours every day post-work. You should be clear about your goals and objectives behind considering a side gig in the first place. Do you have too much debt to pay off? Do you want to fund your child's college expenses? Are you close to retirement and need to boost your savings?

When you know why you want to pursue something, you feel more focused about it. You'll have different timelines for different goals, which is going to help you track your progress. If you don't know the purpose behind desiring to make more money, you'll likely not be able to stay committed to it and may feel frustrated about the whole thing.

Check if You're Allowed to Take Up a Side Gig

If you're working for a company, you need to check with your employer to see if you can pursue a side hustle. It should be mentioned in the employment agreement or you can simply speak with the concerned authority. While most employers don't have any problems with your side hustles—as long as you don't compromise on the quality of work with them—it's still safer to keep things transparent.

Choose the Right Side Hustle

The next step is to figure out what you want to do. You shouldn't rush into starting something and then realize later that it was something you didn't enjoy. While you can experiment with something new, make sure you like it and are comfortable doing it. So, take your time to make an inventory of your hobbies and skills. Now, the tricky part here is that whatever you choose to do should be able to generate money. The best way to ensure that is to ask yourself, "is it going to add value to somebody's life?" If you're capable of doing something that solves a problem and it makes you happy, it's worth doing. For instance, if you love pets and know how to take care of them, you can walk other people's dogs.

Be Conscious of Time Commitment

Whenever you want to start a new task or a project, you need to set aside time to be able to finish it. You don't have to spend 12 or 15 hours a day on something to make extra money. You should treat a side gig like a side gig and allocate a particular time slot for it and stick to it. For instance, you may choose to drive for Uber, but only on the weekends, or teach online on Monday and Thursday evenings between 5 p.m and 7 p.m.

Don't Leave Money on the Table

You should be clear about getting the right price for your service or product. Never hesitate to ask for what you're worth. Remember, when people reach out to you for something that you're an expert at, it's helping them make progress in life. For example, if you're a social media influencer and a brand wants to leverage your popularity and reach out to a certain segment of people, they're supposed to pay you for your clout and expertise.

Make a Slow and Modest Start

Never rush into investing a lot of money in a new business. You should instead make a small start and try to comprehend how things flow with time. The very idea of a side hustle is meant to keep the risk to a minimum. When you make a slow start, you have time to know if you're enjoying what you're doing and if it's something that you'd want to do long-term. More importantly, you should also realize if it's profitable enough to help you sustain yourself even without a job. Thus, it's not wise to quit your day job until you begin earning a steady income from your alternative business. Remember, the regular cash flow is always good—and it's required.

Inventory Your Skill Set

Many people struggle to find out what they're good at. The simplicity of a side hustle is that it can be anything. There are people who love to bake cakes while others are good at organizing and cleaning homes. Some are impressive public speakers and can offer advice on various matters. So, if you know a great deal about a specific topic, you can be a consultant. For instance, there are so many bloggers and YouTubers out there who write or speak about niche subjects and their audiences find value in their content. There are social media influencers who share their knowledge and expertise on how to handle personal finances, how to stay fit and healthy, how to feel motivated every day, how to travel on a low budget, and lots of other topics and genres. If you think you don't have what it takes to write a blog or speak in front of the camera, you can edit videos for others. Beyond that, you can also assist brands with digital marketing and SEO (Search Engine Optimization). You can plan and organize events for others. If you have a knack for graphic designing, you can brush it up and reach out to clients who might need your designing services. As you can see, there are a variety of skills that different people have, which they can use to make some extra money.

After you've listed out your skills, you should consider your strengths. It's equally important to recognize your strengths because they should support your skills. For example, if you're a highly creative product designer but lack time management and negotiation skills, this can keep you from gaining many clients. Thus, you need to combine your skills and strengths to help you move forward with your idea.

Identify a Problem and Define a Solution

Being an entrepreneur starts with the willingness to solve a problem. So, you might have to do some research and talk to people who perhaps have similar interests or work in the same industry. You need to find out what people are struggling with and how you can help them find a solution. For example, if somebody can write a great book but they need someone to edit it for them, and if that's you, it's your chance to monetize it.

In order to understand that somebody has a problem and you're the best person to help them, meaning you have the right skill set to provide a solution, you need to first explore the present scenario deeply. You need to think over the problem and the kind of impact it has on the person in question. For example, if a sustainable clothing brand wants to reach its desired customers, they need to apply appropriate marketing techniques to their business approach. It's not just about making great products, but also knowing how to market them. These are two distinctive areas of expertise. Somebody who is highly skilled at marketing may not have the creativity to make new products and vice versa. There are so many companies who make brilliant products, but they're never picked by buyers. The problem is the lack of clever marketing and promotional ideas. On the other hand, there are brands who make smart marketing campaigns and are able to win people's attention, but their products aren't good enough. So, you need to identify the gap and see if you can fill it.

In another instance, those who babysit or pet sit know that there are people who have busy work schedules and find it challenging to provide quality care to their children and pets. Thus, they hire professionals who can make their lives easier. Without a babysitter or a pet sitter, many people will feel helpless, frustrated, and guilty about not being able to fulfill their duties.

So, you need to find your ideal customer, identify your competitors and learn about their strengths and weaknesses, and see if you have an opportunity in the market.

Putting Your Plan Into Action

Once you've shortlisted your skills and decided on what you want to do, it's time to execute it. Each side hustle has its specific requirements, which you need to ensure. For instance, if you want to rent your car, you need to make sure that it's in good condition and doesn't need a repair. Also, you shouldn't need it for your personal use. Then, you need to set up an account on a car-sharing marketplace.

In another scenario, if you want to sell your writing services, you need to understand how content marketing works, have knowledge of English writing rules, and prepare a portfolio of writing samples to upload on freelance websites like Fiverr and Upwork.

You should keep your side hustle flexible and allow yourself to explore possibilities of turning it into a full-time business. For instance, if you sell self-designed products on Etsy as a side gig, you can consider becoming a digital entrepreneur and setting up your own ecommerce site. Similarly, if you want to make an entry into the arena of vacation rentals, you can test the waters by renting out a spare space or maybe cohost with someone to find out if you enjoy hosting strangers. If yes, you can learn the ropes and make a plan to start your own Airbnb hosting business. You may want to rent a property or buy one, find out about local short-term rental laws, and begin preparing your place for hosting.

When you're ready to call your side hustle a business, you need to give it a name and register it legally. The next step is to price your product and/or service. You need to do some market research and find out what your competitors are charging and also consider the value you're offering. The final step is to find channels of marketing and promotion. You may want to start by spreading the word about your business on social media and then also setting up your own website.

As soon as you get your first paying customer, you have a chance to get feedback and improve upon your business ideas. Then, you should set certain measurable business goals and milestones to grow as an entrepreneur. Once your side hustle becomes a business of its own, you need to learn about taxes. Don't wait for your yearly revenue and profits. Get in touch with a tax professional and understand how taxes work for a business.

A side hustle is a smart way to discover what you truly love doing. The best part is that you can take your time in exploring your own abilities and wait for the right time to scale up the business. In the next chapter, we'll get down to unveiling the fact that accomplishing a business is possible even without a lot of capital investment.

Chapter 9: Low-Cost Business

"Failure isn't fatal, but failure to change might be." –John Wooden

People who turn into entrepreneurs don't necessarily have lots of cash to begin with. All they have are a few skills, but more importantly, the willingness to do something of their own. Anybody can start their own business as long as they have the entrepreneurial spirit and a mindset to grow. When you have the determination, you can learn ways to execute your ideas. Most people are afraid to step out of their conventional jobs and do something on their own because they believe they don't have enough funds. They simply don't want to be in a position where they don't have any financial backup in case their business doesn't work. So, there are all kinds of thoughts and turmoil that people go through while thinking about establishing a business. However, it's a myth that a business has to have high overhead costs. You can come up with a low-cost business idea, too.

Most small businesses do not require too much capital investment in the beginning. You can consider all kinds of service-based ideas instead of product-based businesses. There are so many skills that can be turned into profitable businesses.

Popular Ideas to Start Your Own Business

Below are some of the ideas you can dabble in when you decide to launch a low-cost business:

Event Planning

If you're someone who likes to organize parties, family events, and reunions, you can take it to another level and become an event planner. You can start by reaching out to people on social media and planning events for your friends and acquaintances, who can then spread the word about you by recommending your services to their network.

All you need is attention to detail and the passion to plan events. Of course, you'll need to build a database of vendors, as well, who you'd need for event planning.

Social Media Marketing

Social media is a channel for honest and value-based marketing. Brands are aware that most people rely on social media for various products and services. Therefore, it's important to put into effect strategies to attract the consumers who might be interested in your business. Since social media marketing requires a lot of time and creativity, many big and small companies alike look for social media managers and consultants to handle their social profiles.

A social media consultant or marketeer is well-versed in writing impressive marketing copy, sharing valuable information, and keeping their audience engaged. Their job consists of preparing the entire month's content calendar, creating interesting and fun campaigns, and measuring the growth of their accounts.

Content Creation

We live in the era of the creator economy, where we have the demand of creative professionals like writers and graphic designers. Thus, there's an enormous supply of creative content for various media outlets and businesses. So, you can establish yourself as a service provider of creative services.

Paid Reviewer

Writing honest reviews for a company's products or somebody's books can be a business venture. You don't just get to try a new gadget or read a book, but get paid for it as well. It's not something that requires any investment on your end. All you need to give is your time and apply your skills to review something.

Home-Based Online Educator

There are so many things (web designing, yoga, a new language, or baking) that different people want to learn, but they don't want to take a complicated course or devote too much of their time. Thus, they look for someone who could simplify things for them and give them the option to learn lessons at their own pace. So, you can offer virtual classes, and create PDFs and videos that students can download and watch whenever they want to.

Blogging and Vlogging

While there are so many blogs and vlogs out there, the quality ones get noticed and bring in revenue for the creators. The secret is consistency. If you're passionate about something and can create content around it that people may find interesting, you can monetize it sooner or later. Many videos on YouTube are shot with phone cameras but they provide value to the viewer. You don't have to buy expensive equipment right when you launch something. Play around with your creativity first and then upgrade your business.

Graphic Designing

If you have an eye for designing, you can learn graphic designing skills and design for various products, such as T-shirts, book covers, brochures, display ads, flyers, and logos. You can focus on building your client base in the beginning and then establish it into a business. The only investment you need is a laptop with Photoshop, Illustrator, or Canva installed.

Photography and Videography

In today's age, everybody wants to be spot on with their images and videos they upload on social media. However, not everybody has the creative and technical skills to capture great photos or films. Thus, they don't mind hiring professional photographers and filmmakers for important events like weddings, vacations, baby showers, birthdays, and romantic getaways. So, if you're a talented photographer or videographer, you can help other people make their special days memorable and get paid. All you need is a good camera, a passion for taking pictures, and an interest in meeting new people. If you're skilled only at photography, you can also establish it like a joint venture and rope in somebody who's excellent at shooting videos.

Selling Handmade Products

Creating beautiful products like candles, soaps, and pottery at home is a fun hobby, which can be turned into a lucrative online business. You don't have to invest anything on product manufacturing initially, as you can make it a per-order basis deal or maybe get a few products ready. You'll have to handle shipping and inventory. However, there's no money that you need upfront. You can increase the production as more people begin to buy your goods.

Cleaning Business

Whether it's home or office, every place needs cleaning. Thus, professional cleaners are always in demand. To keep it really low-cost, you can make it a mobile business and operate without an office space. Also, ask your clients to provide their own cleaning supplies. You can put the word out on Facebook and let your contacts know about it. In that way, even marketing it can be quite cost-effective.

However, if you choose to list your services on digital marketplaces like Care.com, Angi, and HomeAdvisor, they charge a nominal fee.

Bookkeeping

While accounting is an integral part of running a business, no business owner likes it. They need somebody reliable and efficient to do the job for them. Thus, you have a chance to offer your bookkeeping services if you're skilled at accounting tasks. The only cost you'll have to bear is buying a bookkeeping software, which largely depends on your client. If they choose to add you as a user on their accounts, you don't have to pay for it either.

Home-Based Bakery

Launching your own restaurant or even food truck can be expensive; however, starting a modest bakery from home can be extremely low-cost. If you really enjoy baking and are confident of making delicious treats, you can set up a small home-based business, which can turn out to be profitable. You can get in touch with local restaurants to stock your items in the beginning, and as your business grows, you can invest in buying a bigger and better oven and other baking equipment.

Meal Planning and Cooking

Eating well is everyone's basic requirement; however, there are a lot of people who don't feel inclined toward preparing healthy meals. Thus, they're happy to pay someone who can plan their meals, meaning they need assistance with creating recipes and learning about nutritive diet plans without spending too much money.

If you've gone to a culinary school or are a hobby chef, you can even cook daily or weekly meals for your customers. The job may require you to visit supermarkets and people's homes, but it can be a well-paying business.

Personal Physical Fitness Coaching

If you're a fitness coach or a yoga expert, you can offer personal training to people remotely or by visiting their homes. You can even set up your own website and social media business profiles to brand yourself as a personal trainer. You can also combine it with advising people on following a healthy diet plan and living a holistically well-balanced life. In addition, you can launch your training programs and online courses on fitness.

Assisting People Virtually

If you're someone who enjoys assisting others and taking care of tasks like replying to emails, fixing appointments, managing calendars, entering data, and offering customer support, you can sell your virtual assistance services to relevant clients. You can find your first client by networking with different people on social media and asking for recommendations. You may have to pay for registration and a certification program; however, there's no real cost involved in establishing yourself as a virtual assistant.

Home Organizing

If you're good at organizing and keeping your home in order, you can probably help others with their homes, too. Your services can include decluttering, rearranging different rooms and stuff, and sorting house items. This business obviously doesn't have a startup cost and you don't need an office space, either.

Funding Your First Business

While you have many low-cost business options to consider, you still need some amount of capital to fund your business requirements. For instance, if you want to open a gym, you are going to need workout equipment. People usually make use of their personal savings to be able to pay for their business operations. However, there are better ways to raise money for your entrepreneurial efforts. The first thing you need to be sure of is the amount you need. You may have to write a business plan on paper, prepare an initial budget, and then draw out an estimate of your overhead costs.

Below are some potential sources of funding for your first business:

Self-Funding

You can self-fund your business' initial operational needs by dipping into your savings or asking one of your family members to lend you some money. However, you should refrain from taking money from your retirement account, as it may lead to early withdrawal penalties or charges.

Credit Unions and Banks

You may want to go to traditional financial institutions, such as credit unions and banks for loans. Just like you'd borrow money for buying a car or a house, you will need to take credit for business purposes. You can avail quite a big amount, but the approval process can take time. Also, they might want to be sure of your business plan and demand collateral.

Crowdfunding

You can also raise money through crowdfunding, which is asking for donations from a huge number of people. The benefit to a business owner is that they don't have to pay the crowdfunders their money back or give them any share in the business ownership. The money that crowdfunders contribute isn't considered an investment; thus, they're not eligible for any financial return. They simply receive a gift or some merchandise once the business takes off. However, you should read the documents of the crowdfunding platform you choose before taking up this option.

Online Lenders

Online lenders can be private companies or businesses that specialize in online lending. Apart from that, even banks, CDFIs, and SBA-backed lenders lend money to new business owners via online platforms. It's definitely a quick and easy option for business owners because they don't have to go through lengthy application processes and don't have to wait too long for approval. That said, the non-bank online lenders typically charge higher interest fees and penalties. So, you need to understand the repayment terms carefully before signing the deal.

Venture Capital

You can get access to venture capital from investors to fund your new business. In this type of a deal, investors get a share in the company ownership and involvement in decision-making. Therefore, it's not a loan that you get from investors, but it's a long-term investment on their part. However, venture capitalists look for high growth companies and they want to be part of the board of directors.

It's important to find an investor who has a good track record of making investments in various new companies. Before investing in your business, they're going to review your business plan, marketing strategies, products, and management.

Mission-Driven Lenders

If you need guidance and mentorship along with funding, you can go with mission-driven lenders, such as community development financial institutions (CDFIs). They might not lend you a huge amount of money like banks, but it's a valuable opportunity for inexperienced entrepreneurs to learn about various aspects of business operations.

SBA Investment Programs

You can opt for SBA investment programs to get funds for your business. There are SBICs (Small Business Investment Companies) who offer both equity and debt investment to small businesses by utilizing their own fund along with an SBA guaranteed borrowed capital.

Then, there's the Small Business Innovation Research (SBIR) program that offers a platform to small businesses for federal research and development, which may lead to funding.

You can also consider applying for the Small Business Technology Transfer (STTR) program that may open doors for capital opportunities in the federal innovation research and development field. If you qualify for this program, you get to work with nonprofit research institutions in the beginning and thereafter while you're still quite new in the arena of entrepreneurship.

Credit Cards

You can use the credit available on your credit card to fund your business's operational requirements and pay it back the way you normally do. Yes, you need to be aware of the interest charges and ensure that you get a favorable rate to reduce the debt. Although the amount that you get to use with a credit card isn't as high as that of a bank loan, it's still a simpler process. You don't need anybody's approval for anything. It can be a suitable funding option for small businesses.

Friends and Family

If you don't want to go through the process of applying for loans and figuring out different terms of different professional lenders, you can also consider asking for financial aid from your close friends or family. It's an easy and simple deal as long as you share a bond of mutual trust with the other person. While there's a risk of losing money for the lender, they also have a chance to make some money if the business succeeds.

Scaling Your Business

To scale your business is to increase the bandwidth to manage the growing sales, the work needed to be done, and the output. If you don't have a scalability plan in place, you may not be able to deal with the increasing demand of your product. There are small companies that grow quite fast and begin to make profits early; however, they aren't able to sustain themselves because they haven't scaled their business.

Scaling your business isn't growing your business. When you scale your business, you help it retain its growth. For instance, if you start a small bakery with one or two staff who work in the kitchen, and it begins to receive massive demand for cakes within a short span of time, you will need to hire more staff to handle increased sales.

Here's how you can scale your business:

Keep Milestones in Mind

Every business should have certain milestones to reach. You should correlate the need for capital with your company's growth stages. Try to gauge the stage when you'll require more funds, and set milestones accordingly. You should have clarity on how soon you want to achieve your targets, so that you have a specific budget in place and have time for sourcing capital whenever the need arises.

Build Your Team

You need to have efficient and reliable personnel in place to carry out all the operations smoothly and to deal with growing customer demand. There are different aspects to a business, such as genuinely helpful customer support, highly-skilled technology professionals, and an effective sales and marketing staff.

However, that's just one part of building your team. You also need to nurture relationships with people who help you run your business, such as your partners, suppliers, patrons, and also your customers. A loyal customer can bring so many more new customers to your business and contribute to your growth.

Ensure Your Product/Service Is Excellent

Never make the mistake of trying to sell something that's not up to the mark and needs improvement or changes. Some business owners think that they can work on their products once they begin receiving more profits; however, the best time to ensure your product quality is right when you start. The early days of business should be about taking customer feedback and making sure that your product meets their expectations. The more you focus on providing high quality products and services to your clients, the higher growth your business will have.

Assure Your Investors and Customers of the Company's Ongoing Growth

You should maintain a transparent relationship with your investors and customers in order to keep their trust in your business. Your potential investors may want to know about the number of recent customers. Also, your customers should also have a chance to see how many other people are using your products, so that they gain more confidence in the quality of your creation.

Maintain Smooth Internal Processes and Operations

A sustainable business isn't just about success that's seen on the outside, but also about how things work behind the scenes, which is a company's internal processes and systems. If the infrastructure of a company is inefficient in some way, it's going to impact sales sooner or later. It's the core of your business growth in the long run. While you won't be able to bring in everything on a large scale in the beginning and might have to be flexible with how you want to operate, developing a certain framework is vital. Of course, you can always build upon what you already have, but you can't go back and correct what's already messed up.

Make Use of Smart Tools and Technology

You need to incorporate the required tools and technology for smooth and fast communication between your teams and also ensure hassle-free customer interaction. While there are video conferencing and phone options, it's better to have a unified communication system, which can be in the form of an app.

Then, you need a customer relationship management (CRM) system to store all your client information in one place, and if you can integrate your CRM with your communication app, it would be even better. You should also get workflow automation software, which reduces the time consumed in repetitive tasks and boosts productivity of your staff.

Don't Focus on Selling

The biggest mistake you can make as a new business owner is trying to sell your product blatantly. The right approach is to make sure that your product is so good that it sells itself. You need to educate and instigate your target customers to want to buy your products. Thus, you need to market at the right places, meaning you need to be aware of where your desired customers hang out. If they read blogs, you should have content marketing and SEO in place. If they check out products on social media, you should create engaging posts to hold their interest.

So, focus on understanding your ideal client's needs and delivering the best product before hiring a sales team.

Build Your Brand Image

Marketing and promoting your product and or service is different from shaping your brand image. Your ideal customers should know you for something specific that only you can offer. It could be your high quality products, superior customer service, and something different that your competitors miss out on. You need to position your brand in a certain way for your desired clients to notice you. For instance, if you've started a new coffee shop that serves coffee that's prepared while keeping the environment in mind, you should let your customers know about it.

You need to tell your brand story and educate people on how your company cares about sustainability and wouldn't do anything to harm the environment. By setting a certain standard of what you offer to your customers, you set the right expectations for the kind of people you choose to work with. Everybody from the design, marketing, and sales team will know how to operate so that your vision comes across clearly through each customer interaction.

Scaling a business can be hard, but if you have a solid business strategy in place and work with the right tools and people, your business will continue to thrive. You need to understand the difference between massive growth and sustainable growth. If you aim for the latter, you'll always be on the right track.

So, you can have a business idea and take it off the ground without a significant financial investment. However, if you need to fund your business at some point, earlier or later, you can reach out to one of the lending platforms or institutions. Also, you should be prepared to scale your business before it gets too overwhelming to manage. If you do everything step-by-step and are adaptable and innovative, you can establish yourself as a successful entrepreneur.

In the next chapter, we'll touch upon a strategy that's going to help you reach the pinnacle of financial freedom and stay there.

Chapter 10: Passive Income

"You become financially free when your passive income exceeds your expenses." –T. Harv Eker

What if you make money regularly without really working? Is it even possible? Yes, it is. We call this "passive" income. Anyone can create a source of cash flow for themselves by offering other people something of value. If you've created a blog, which manages to pull lots of traffic because of its informative content, you can make money even while sleeping by placing ads and affiliate links on it. Similarly, if you've bought a house, which you've rented out to somebody, you're making money passively. Anything that you do without putting in effort and giving your time, which still produces money for you, is deemed passive income. It can be your valuable assets, such as property, stocks, or a business that you're not actively part of. Remember, it's not your second job or a part-time hustle because you do need to work actively to make money through them.

Although passive income doesn't demand your time and effort as much as an active income does, it's not something that comes without any investment. In fact, the luxury and comfort of drawing an income without active work is

the result of a person's investment of their time, money, and applying their mental labor. It takes time to reach a position when you can enjoy the growth in the assets you can call your own. If you purchase a property, you need to save plenty of money for its down payment and also pay the mortgage fees later each month to be able to earn rental income out of it eventually. When you buy individual stocks, you need to study the company you want to invest in and keep your money blocked for a period of time to be able to gain some returns later.

It's important to know that passive income isn't free money or something easy to achieve. You need to work your way through the entire process and be actively involved in building an asset first before you can expect it to become an income-generating machine for you.

Why You Should Aim for Passive Income

The purpose of passive income is to set you free from the obligation of going to the office every day and giving your time to a job that you probably do not like much. It gives you the choice to quit your job if you aren't happy and do something that fulfills you. When you feel a sense of freedom and realize you have more choices in life, you can make better decisions for yourself. You feel more alive and ready to take on any challenge. You can take up a new hobby and see if it gives you joy. You don't have to work for money anymore because it's coming to you anyway. With passive income in your pocket, you can live financially free and have the peace that you'll be able to fund whatever you need in life. You can move to a new city and live there for a while or travel indefinitely without seeking anyone's permission.

Passive income allows you to live debt-free, pay all your bills on time, take care of all your living expenses, and plan a future. When your finances are right, they have a positive impact on your physical and mental health. Not just that, but even your relationships blossom because you're able to devote more time to understanding the other person's needs and reciprocating their love.

The best part is that you'll never feel the need to buy things on credit or take on more debt. You'll be able to accomplish all your life milestones (higher education, marriage, moving into a bigger house, and starting a family) and fulfill all your long-forgotten dreams (solo vacationing in the European countryside, writing a book, or helping a charity) with the money that you know will arrive because you have an appreciating asset.

Passive income also enables you to maintain your desired lifestyle even when inflation is increasing at a high pace and all goods and services are getting costlier by the day. Of course, it has to be a high return asset, such as real estate or a business to earn you significant passive income. While many things can earn you passive income, they might not buy you everything you seek. For instance, if you've written an ebook and it's bought by only a few people, it's not going to contribute much to your life. So, it depends on what kind of asset you create and how much passive earning you can manage to generate. If you invest in the right asset, there's no limit to how much you can earn.

Well, it may all sound too good to be true. But such is passive income! If you decide to go down that path, you can live life on your own terms. It's not something reserved for certain privileged people. Everybody can create sources of passive earnings as long as they're willing to explore and experiment with new ventures. You need to open your mind to new ideas and step out to do what has the potential to earn you money in the long run.

Passive Income Strategies

There are different ways to create passive income. It's up to you what you'd like to lay your hands on—investing, asset building, or asset sharing. You can also pick all these options in your own small way and then build upon them. You don't have to feel intimidated about buying expensive assets, such as real estate, if you don't know much about them. While real estate can prove to be one of the most lucrative investments, you should do what you're convinced and capable of and not what everybody else seems to choose.

You need to understand that you can create passive income by investing money as well as investing your time and skills. There are ways to generate passive income even when you don't have money to invest. So, there's no excuse for you to not try it.

Let's look into some of the passive income strategies you can explore:

- You can invest small portions of your monthly income in the stock market with a long-term view. Now, there are multiple ways you can do that—you can buy individual stocks or invest in ETFs and index funds. The money you make through the stock market is in the form of interest payments, capital gains, and regular dividend payments.

• You can purchase properties for the purpose of earning rental income on a regular basis.

• You can also share your existing financial assets, such as renting out an extra room in your apartment, offering your car for rental use, or allowing advertising on your vehicle and making passive money.

• There are many smaller ways to make passive income, such as keeping money in a high-yield savings account for a really long time, which can earn you a reasonably good amount of interest, as well as cash back from credit cards, and using cash back apps.

Passive Income Ideas

Below are some of the ways that require you to invest capital to be able to generate passive income:

Buy Rental Properties

Renting out your property can earn you a regular monthly income, which can be absolutely passive in nature. Of course, you'll have to shell out time to take care of your property by checking if it requires repair work or upgrades. Besides, there are a few ongoing costs like property taxes and homeowner's association fees that you'll have to pay. However, it's largely a profitable passive mode of business.

You can also purchase a property with the perspective of using it as a short-term rental, which can maximize your earning opportunities. You can expand your business by buying multiple properties as you move along in your journey of being a vacation rental owner.

Invest in Dividend Stocks

People who make consistent investments into dividend stocks can accumulate an attractive residual income over time. Dividend stocks are regular payouts that shareholders receive from the company's profits. However, dividend investing isn't devoid of risks. If the stock that you invest in falls in value, the company will not be able to pay you anything. Therefore, you need to choose your dividend stocks carefully and try to pick selective stocks or dividend aristocrats to increase chances of higher dividend yields.

Invest in REITs or Real Estate Crowdfunding

There are alternative ways to own real estate, which are much more cost-effective and simpler than buying physical real estate. If you don't have funds to make an outright purchase or pay for a down payment of a property, you can buy REITs (Real Estate Investment Trusts) just like you'd buy a stock. By investing in a REIT, you gain fractional ownership in the properties listed on the fund. There are residential, retail, office, mortgage, and healthcare REITs that allow investors to earn a significant return over a long-term.

Then, you can also explore real estate crowdfunding, which enables investors to participate in raising capital for building infrastructure and gain from the profits earned. The benefit is that you don't have to contribute a huge sum of money to be able to invest. It's a pool of small investors that connect with companies who need capital to invest in real estate.

Peer-to-Peer Lending

You can make money without much effort by lending money to people who may be in need of significant capital. The lending and borrowing take place on a platform like Prosper. The money that you loan earns interest for you, which can be higher than what a savings account would give you. However, you may also lose your money if the person who you lent money to defaults. Thus, you should lend money to multiple borrowers instead of just one or two of them. To qualify for lending your money, you need to meet certain income requirements.

Silent Partnership in a Business

If you believe in a business idea but don't want to take any operational control, you can simply become a silent partner and invest money. You don't have to take the pain of running the business or dealing with issues because your involvement in the company is passive. Since you've invested a certain amount of capital, you can expect to be part of the profits earned by the company. However, you'll also be part of the losses if the business doesn't grow.

Build CD Ladders

You can buy CDs (certificates of deposits) from banks and build a CD Ladder. Since they are a low risk investment, their returns are also low. However, you can buy them in certain increments to be able to earn higher returns.

Buy Individual Stocks

Investing in individual stocks is just like being a silent partner in a company. You need to buy stock of a company that you like and believe is going to make profits. If the stock value goes up, you also earn a profit, and if it declines, you also lose money. Picking individual stocks is highly risky and it's certainly not suitable for new and inexperienced investors. The safer approach to stock market investing is mutual funds, ETFs (exchange traded funds), or index funds. These funds have multiple stocks listed under them, which allows enough diversification and the risk of loss is reduced to a great extent.

The above methods can be great ways to make your money produce more money for you; however, if you're hesitant to invest, you can pick "no cost" ideas of inventing passive income streams. Let's take a look at some of them:

Launch a YouTube Channel

YouTubers who pass a certain benchmark of viewership are easily able to make somewhere around $60,000 per year. But, of course, it doesn't start on that high of a note. There's lots of hard work, creativity, and consistency required to reach that level. If you're someone who loves to be in front of the camera and has a niche subject to talk about, YouTube can be a great "passive income" platform for you. People make money with ad placement, affiliate links, and sponsorships. You obviously need to create a lot of great quality content for a period of time before you can make money in your sleep. The videos that you upload will continue to be there and keep generating an income via affiliate sales and ads.

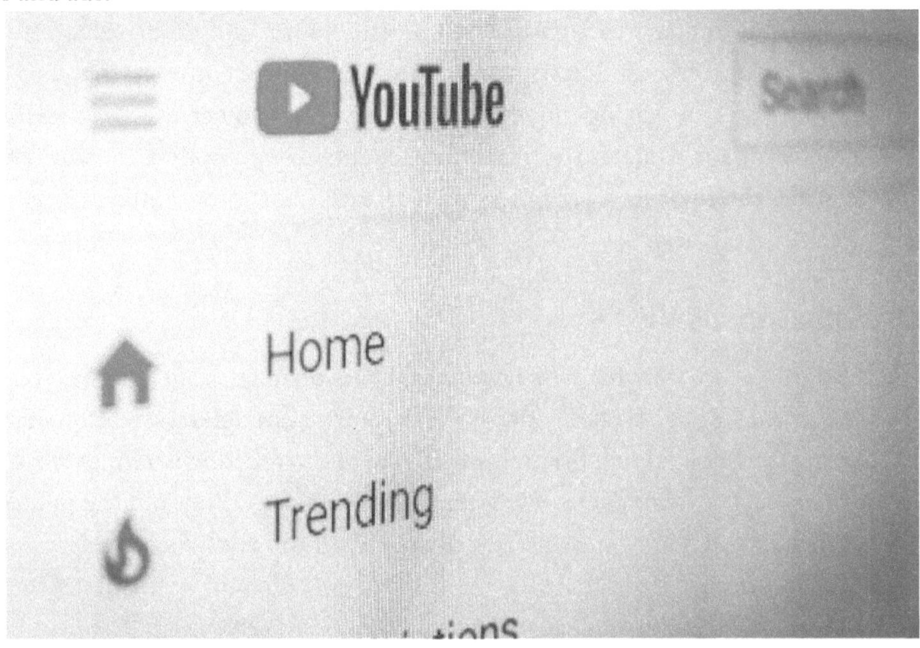

Start a Blog

Bloggers can make money in so many different ways, such as display ads, affiliate links, sponsored posts, branded content, and product sales. Be aware that there's typically no income for a new blog. You'll need to write a lot of articles on your blog on a regular basis to be able to monetize it. Apart from creating valuable content, you'll need to implement SEO strategies and constantly work on building your network.

Create an Online Course

If you're a subject matter expert, create a course and sell it online. If you're an established YouTuber or a blogger, it's going to be much easier to attract buyers for your course. The only criteria for selecting your course subject is that it should offer value to your target customers. You need to find out the topics people are looking up on search engines and social media. For instance, people usually want to make money out of a hobby but they don't know how to execute the idea. So, if you know the tactics to convert a passion into a profitable business, you can share your in-depth knowledge and insights and help others reach their goals.

You can prepare written material, record audio, and shoot videos of your course lessons. It's also important to price your course correctly. If you price it too low, you'll be leaving money on the table, and if you charge too much, you may discourage some of the potential students from enrolling in your course. To strike the right balance, you should research how other online courses are priced in the market.

Write a Book/Ebook

If you have the flair for writing and feel passionately about a topic, you can write a book or ebook and earn passive income. Although researching, writing, getting the book edited, finding a publisher, and marketing is a lot of work and involves an initial financial investment of paying the editor and the publisher, it can earn you handsome royalties all your life if the book succeeds.

You can also take the easier and more cost-effective path of writing an ebook and self-publishing it on Amazon, which is a zero-cost investment.

Showcase Your Photography Online

If you can take high-quality photographs and have the right equipment, you can build a bank of relevant images and upload it on stock photography websites like Shutterstock, Alamy, or Getty Images to create opportunities for passive income. Each time someone buys your photograph, you earn a certain percentage of it. Since your image can be downloaded several times, it becomes your passive income over time. You'll need to research the kind of images clients look for, so that you can fulfill the demand of highly searched images.

Social Media Campaigns

It's an age of social media marketing and there are barely any brands who're oblivious of its benefits. So, if you're someone who loves to be on social media and interact with new people, you can create a cohesive profile and build your presence. Social media influencers who have a huge number of followers and a high engagement rate are able to make a significant amount of money each month with brand partnerships. Just like blogging and video-making, building your social media profile is hard work, but it pays off exceedingly well if you manage to create meaningful content with a certain audience base in mind. You need to discover what you're passionate about and then work on becoming its representative.

For instance, if you're a fitness freak, you can post content related to fitness and inspire people to incorporate fitness into their lifestyle. As a result, you can partner with brands that sell fitness products and create marketing campaigns for them. This can turn into easy money, as there are several campaigns that simply require you to post a video or image given by the brand with just a few hashtags.

Turn Your Extra Room Into an Airbnb

If you have a room that you rarely use, it's an opportunity for passive income. All you need to do is declutter it, remove your personal belongings, and set it up for your guests. Take some nice pictures of the space and upload it on Airbnb's platform, write a description, mention the amenities, set the pricing, and you're ready to receive your first guests. You can manage your calendar and ensure that you do not receive any unwanted bookings. It's a flexible way of generating additional income without much effort.

However, you must check the local short-term rental laws and regulations before creating your account on Airbnb.

Start a Podcast

People listen to podcasts when they are jogging, driving to work, cooking, or simply lounging in their living rooms. You don't have to read or watch something with undivided focus to understand it, but you can go about your day and still find lots of value by simply listening to audio. So, if you can share your expertise on a subject and inspire people to take the right action to improve their lives, you can win subscribers, which can turn into a great earning opportunity. You can have ad partners sponsor your shows, and you can even connect with podcast advertising networks.

Launch Your Own Job Board

You can also set up your own job board online and make a passive income out of it. All you need to do is buy a domain and a hosting plan, which isn't a large investment, and allow employers to display job vacancies for job searchers to see. As a result, you can charge employers for posting on your job board. You can also give them premium features like sponsored jobs or allow them to access your candidate database as many times as they need to.

There are many resources available these days and lots of networking platforms for you to connect with people. You can find your own path to passive income. If you have capital to invest, make sure you evaluate the risk factor before you decide on an undertaking.

Also, be aware that passive income is taxable. However, it's not taxed like your regular income. You need to understand how you need to pay taxes for a passive income that you make depending on the kind of business you do. For example, your rental income is taxed as ordinary income, but you can claim deductions for the mortgage interest and other expenses. So, there are different rules and regulations to follow when it comes to how you need to pay taxes for your passive income. The best approach is to contact a tax professional and take their advice as to how to deal with taxes and retain most of your earnings.

Passive income is a treasure that you should try to find early in life. However, if you still have only one source of income, you can start today. It's never too late to make the decision and begin taking action toward your financial independence.

Conclusion

Since you've reached the end of the book, you now have the key to unlocking your financial destiny. Creating wealth isn't something you can accomplish in a day. It's about consistent financial discipline and being goal-driven about your life, which each come from financial awareness. The number one cause of people's financial distress is a lack of knowledge on money matters. The moment you begin to think about money in a positive way and believe that it's in your hands to make it right, you get on the path of wealth building.

The first thing you need to address is how you treat money. Money management is a skill that anyone can develop as long as they're willing and want to improve their finances. Good finances are not about how well paid you are, but how well you handle your money—using credit cards to your advantage and not getting in debt can contribute to your financial progress. You don't have to feel subjugated by money, but make every dollar work for you. Once you learn simple money-saving skills like budgeting and tracking your expenses, you can explore various investment options to make your money grow. From stocks, mutual funds, real estate, to cryptocurrency, there are a ton of different ways to give your money the chance to appreciate over time. However, you need to set certain financial milestones to be able to work toward them. If you save and invest money without any clarity about your purpose in life, you'll not know what to do and how to do it. You may pick an asset class and then leave it whenever you feel demotivated by market volatility. However, when you know you want to have a big nest egg for your life after you quit working, you'll have the courage to keep going with the investment. You need to keep in mind that investing is the game of patience, discipline, and diversification. It needs strategies and commitment for a long period of time. If you learn it early on, you can set yourself up for surpassing inflation in every decade.

In addition to savings and investments, you also need to think of creating additional income sources, such as a side hustle or two, a low-cost business, and a source of passive income. Most people are afraid to make investments thinking they're too risky, but money isn't the only capital that you need for creating wealth. You can also invest your time, knowledge, and resources to make money. There are so many entrepreneurial opportunities available, meaning there are many problems you can solve for other people. There are so many ways you can add value to their lives. You need to think like an investor and not someone who's merely trying their luck in the market.

The more money you make, the more financial stability you have. You can live without debt, feel more peaceful, create more opportunities for yourself, and afford everything you ever desired. More importantly, you live an inspiring life that others want to emulate.

Being wealthy isn't about owning a lot of expensive things—it's about gaining financial confidence that you can face uncertainty and still be okay. People who're truly wealthy never work for money. They work for happiness and fulfillment. They're able to identify their dreams and goals. They don't need validation from their peers or bosses for who they are and what they want to do, which is why they're able to get out of the paycheck-to-paycheck cycle and discover their own path of generating income.

If you seriously apply the financial roadmap and principles offered in this book, you will definitely get on the path of building wealth and financial freedom. Remember, money is just a tool meant for people to use. You have the power to create money and also make it work for you all your life.

Hopefully, this book has helped you find a perspective, and you feel motivated to start a new relationship with your finances, which doesn't consist of fear and worry, but of hope and confidence. It would be great if you could leave a review so that others who have similar struggles to you can also benefit from this book.

References

5 reasons why passive income is important. (2016, August 30). Wanderlust Worker. https://www.wanderlustworker.com/5-reasons-why-passive-income-is-important/

Blumberg, Y. (2018, September 29). *The top 7 sacrifices Americans are making to get richer.* CNBC. https://www.cnbc.com/2018/09/28/top-7-sacrifices-americans-are-making-to-get-richer.html

Boyte-White, C. (2021, June 28). *How to choose an online stock broker.* Investopedia. https://www.investopedia.com/investing/complete-guide-choosing-online-stock-broker/

Brock, C. (2022, June 8). *What is passive income?* The Motley Fool. https://www.fool.com/investing/how-to-invest/passive-income/

Cabler, J. (2015, December 3). *9 Financial discipline tips that will make you rich. Celebrating Financial Freedom.* https://www.cfinancialfreedom.com/9-financial-discipline-tips-make-you-rich/

Caginalp, R. (2022, September 12). *How to acquire and establish a rental property.* Bankrate. https://www.bankrate.com/mortgages/how-to-establish-a-rental-property/

Chen, J. (2003, November 25). *Passive income.* Investopedia. https://www.investopedia.com/terms/p/passiveincome.asp

Cruze, R. (2022, April 25). *How to set financial goals.* Ramsey Solutions. https://www.ramseysolutions.com/personal-growth/setting-financial-goals

Daly, L. (2021, October 26). *How to safely store cryptocurrency.* The Motley Fool. https://www.fool.com/investing/stock-market/

market-sectors/financials/cryptocurrency-stocks/how-to-store-cryptocurrency/

Davey, L. (2022, July 8). *What is passive income? [Definition + Guide for 2022]*. Shopify. https://www.shopify.com/blog/passive-income

DiLallo, M. (2020, November 24). *Why is it important to invest in stocks?* The Motley Fool. https://www.fool.com/investing/how-to-invest/stocks/why-invest-in-stocks/

Esajian, P. (2021, October 26). *How to invest in cryptocurrency: A beginner's guide.* FortuneBuilders. https://www.fortunebuilders.com/how-to-invest-in-cryptocurrency/

Farrington, R. (2022, September 2). *5 benefits of investing.* The college investor. https://thecollegeinvestor.com/16912/5-benefits-of-investing/

Fontinelle, A. (2021, March 29). *Setting financial goals for your future.* Investopedia. https://www.investopedia.com/articles/personal-finance/100516/setting-financial-goals/

Fund your business. (2019). U.S. small business administration. https://www.sba.gov/business-guide/plan-your-business/fund-your-business

Hayden, B. (2016, January 18). *5 keys to turning your side hustle into a successful business.* Entrepreneur. https://www.entrepreneur.com/starting-a-business/5-keys-to-turning-your-side-hustle-into-a-successful/254192

How to start budgeting for investing. (n.d.). www.bitpanda.com. https://www.bitpanda.com/academy/en/lessons/how-to-start-budgeting-for-investing/

If you spend more than you earn | Budgeting | GetSmarterAboutMoney.ca. (2017, June 16). GetSmarterAboutMoney.ca. https://www.getsmarteraboutmoney.ca/plan-manage/planning-basics/budgeting/if-you-spend-more-than-you-earn/

Jackson, T. (2021, December 13). *How to effectively manage & pay off credit card debt.* InCharge Debt Solutions. https://www.incharge.org/understanding-debt/credit-card/how-to-manage-credit-card-debt/

Jake. (2021, January 31). *Self-Discipline: The key to building wealth.* Wealthy Corner. https://www.wealthycorner.com/self-discipline-the-key-to-building-wealth/

Jespersen, C. (2020, December 15). *5 steps for tracking your monthly expenses.* NerdWallet. https://www.nerdwallet.com/article/finance/tracking-monthly-expenses

Kantrowitz, M. (2020, November 6). *How to get your spending under control.* Forbes. https://www.forbes.com/sites/markkantrowitz/2020/11/06/how-to-get-your-spending-under-control/?sh=207869a23d40

Lake, R. (2021, September 30). *Why you should be monitoring your checking account regularly.* Investopedia. https://www.investopedia.com/how-often-should-you-monitor-your-checking-account-4798537

Langager, C. (2019). *A beginner's guide to stock investing.* Investopedia. https://www.investopedia.com/articles/basics/06/invest1000.asp

Lau, G. (n.d.). *4 tips for scaling a business from real-life businesses.* Dialpad. https://www.dialpad.com/blog/how-to-scale-a-business/

Nover, A. (2019, April 26). *15 things people sacrifice to become rich.*
Medium.   https://medium.com/@auranover/15-things-people-
sacrifice-to-become-rich-345fc35b609a

O'Shea, A., & Davis, C. (2022, August 31). *How to invest in stocks:
A   step-by-step   for   beginners.*   NerdWallet.
https://www.nerdwallet.com/article/investing/
how-to-invest-in-stocks

Peek, S. (2022, June 29). *25 low-cost business ideas -
businessnewsdaily.com.*   Business   News   Daily.
https://www.businessnewsdaily.com/5767-business-ideas-low-
cost.html

Pofeldt, E. (2021, January 27). *The ultimate side hustle guide for
2021.* CNBC. https://www.cnbc.com/guide/side-hustles/

Prater, M. (2019, June 19). *Scaling your business: 6 stages you need
to know.* Blog.hubspot.com.   https://blog.hubspot.com/sales/
scaling-your-business

Pyles, S. (2021, December 22). *How to get out of credit card debt:
A 4-step guide.* NerdWallet. https://www.nerdwallet.com/article/
finance/
credit-card-debt#:~:text=Pay%20more%20than%20minimum

Reinicke, C. (2022, May 20). *Here's what to consider before starting
a side hustle.* CNBC. https://www.cnbc.com/2022/05/20/heres-
what-to-consider-before-staring-a-side-hustle.html

Robbins, T. (2017, July 3). *11 proven steps to scale a business
successfully* | Tony   Robbins.   Tonyrobbins.com.
https://www.tonyrobbins.com/career-business/mindful-scaling/

Rohde, J. (2022, August 22). *How to buy your first rental property in 2022: 5 simple steps.* Learn.roofstock.com. https://learn.roofstock.com/blog/how-to-buy-rental-property

Seven business funding options and advice — Nationwide. (2020). Nationwide.com. https://www.nationwide.com/lc/resources/small-business/articles/business-funding-options

Sokunbi, B. (2022, March 24). *7 steps for starting a side hustle.* Clever Girl Finance. https://www.clevergirlfinance.com/blog/starting-a-side-hustle/

Sutariya, V. (2021, July 10). *Getting wealthy vs staying wealthy -The Psychology of Money.* www.linkedin.com. https://www.linkedin.com/pulse/getting-wealthy-vs-staying-the-psychology-money-vishal-sutariya-#:~:text=Getting%20money%20requires%20taking%20risks

Top 5 reasons why investing is important. (2022, July 20). Dividend Earner. https://dividendearner.com/why-investing-is-important/#3-top-5-reasons

Tretina, K. (2021, July 12). *How to buy cryptocurrency.* Forbes Advisor. https://www.forbes.com/advisor/investing/cryptocurrency/how-to-buy-cryptocurrency/

The ultimate guide to passive income [25+ strategies that work] – RLT Finance. (n.d.). Road Less Traveled Finance. Retrieved November 16, 2022, from https://roadlesstraveledfinance.com/guide-passive-income/

Which investments have the highest historical returns? (2022, September 29). Investopedia. https://www.investopedia.com/ask/answers/032415/which-investments-have-highest-historical-returns.asp

Whiteside, E. (2019). *What is the 50/20/30 budget rule?* Investopedia. https://www.investopedia.com/ask/answers/022916/what-502030-budget-rule.asp

Williams, S. (n.d.). *The beginner's guide to buying rental properties (A case study).* REtipster. Retrieved November 16, 2022, from https://retipster.com/how-to-buy-rental-properties/

Work to learn, don't work for money. (n.d.). Elearnmarkets. https://www.elearnmarkets.com/school/units/rich-dad-poor-dad/work-to-learn-don-t-work-for-money

Work to learn, don't work for money. (2020, October 25). The Social Comment. https://www.thesocialcomment.com/blog/Work-to-Learn-Dont-Work-for-Money?pid=5f954ead2855104bda2db33c

Image References

Blue and white visa card on silver laptop. (2020). [Unsplash]. https://unsplash.com/photos/s8F8yglbpjo

Distel, A. (2019). Turned-on MacBook Pro [Unsplash]. https://unsplash.com/photos/DfjJMVhwH_8

Eliason, K. (2018). 5 U.S. dollar banknote [Unsplash]. https://unsplash.com/photos/4N3iHYmqy_E

Franta, T. (2018). Person using laptop on white wooden table [Unsplash]. https://unsplash.com/photos/iusJ25iYu1c

George, R. (2020). White and brown house near green grass field under white clouds [Unsplash]. https://unsplash.com/photos/9gGvNWBeOq4

Hearing, P. (2019). Trees beside white house [Unsplash]. https://unsplash.com/photos/IYfp2Ixe9nM

Kanchanara. (2021). All crypto coins are together in the dark [Unsplash]. https://unsplash.com/photos/fsSGgTBoX9Y

Kent, T. (2019). Gray wooden house [Unsplash]. https://unsplash.com/photos/178j8tJrNlc

Mayo, J. (2020a). Macbook pro on a brown wooden table [Unsplash]. https://unsplash.com/photos/NfOKSTutAYk

Mayo, J. (2020b). Person holding black android smartphone [Unsplash]. https://unsplash.com/photos/obJBg2lZjMg

McKenzie, A. (2018). Gold-colored Bitcoin [Unsplash]. https://unsplash.com/photos/iGYiBhdNTpE

Micheile. (2020). Green plant in a clear glass cup [Unsplash]. https://unsplash.com/photos/SoT4-mZhyhE

Mils, A. (2019). Fan of 100 U.S. dollar banknotes [Unsplash]. https://unsplash.com/photos/lCPhGxs7pww

Morrison, N. (2017). MacBook Pro near white open book [Unsplash]. https://unsplash.com/photos/FHnnjk1Yj7Y

Neel, A. (2017). MacBook Pro, white ceramic mug and black smartphone on table [Unsplash]. https://unsplash.com/photos/cckf4TsHAuw

Sampson, G. (2016). Black and white hustle-printed ceramic mug on table [Unsplash]. https://unsplash.com/photos/CmF_5GYc6c0

Sankowski, D. (2016). Flat ray photography book, pencil, camera, and lens [Unsplash]. https://unsplash.com/photos/3OiYMgDKJ6k

Wiediger, C. (2018). Youtube application screengrab [Unsplash]. https://unsplash.com/photos/NmGzVG5Wsg8

Winkler, M. (2020). Green and white typewriter on black textile [Unsplash]. https://unsplash.com/photos/44QtHj3fZDY

◇◇. (2020). Person holding 100 U.S. Dollar banknote [Unsplash]. https://unsplash.com/photos/xBuu23uxarU